I0476823

The Aloepreneur Lifestyle

A book for people who

want more than just a paycheck

FIRST EDITION

YARA LOUA

Mr. Loua is an independent contractor with FLP. The advice and methods expressed in this book represent the opinion of the author and are not necessarily a reflection of methods endorsed by FLP. There are thousands of independent contractor within FLP, each with the right to build his or her business as they fit within guidelines set by FLP. This is one man's story.

Disclaimer

The information contained in this book is provided for general information purposes only and does not constitute medical, legal or other professional advice on any subject matter. The author of this book does not accept any responsibility for loss which may arise from reliance on information contained within this book or any associated websites. The author of this book is NOT a licensed medical doctor and makes no claims to be. The products discussed are not intended to diagnose, mitigate, treat, cure or prevent a specific disease or class of diseases. You should consult your family physician if you are experiencing a medical problem. Any earnings portrayed in this book are not necessarily representative of the income that an individual can or will earn through his or her participation in the marketing plan. All references to income are for illustrative purposes only. Your level of income will be determined by your effort, participation and dedication in building your own business. These figures should NOT be considered as guarantees or projections of your actual earnings.

To the women and men living the Aloepreneur Lifestyle

Contents

Preface

Me: Ring ring…ring ring… ring ring.

Yara: Hello, Yara speaking. How may I help you today?

Me: Yes. This is _____calling. I heard about the book *"The Aloepreneur Lifestyle"* and I would like to know more about it?

Yara: Sure! May I ask you a few questions?

Me: Yes.

Yara: How did you hear about the book?

Me: My friend recommended it to me.

Yara: Okay. Wonderful! What did your friend say about this book?

Me: My friend said the book could help me achieve FREEDOM. She also said I can feel better and look better. I can retire in less than five years, I can have more control over my life, spend more time with my family, be in charge of my own time, work from home and make a lot of money. That sounded too good to be true and I wanted to make sure it's not one of those "PYRAMID SCHEME". Because I am a little bit skeptical of the whole home-based business opportunity. That's the reason I decided to call before buying this book.

Yara: Thanks for calling us! I understand your feelings and it's normal to feel so. Most people feel happy to do the same things day after day because those are the things they know best. Often, they resist trying new things because of the fear of the unknown. Let me give you an illustration: How was your first driving lesson and experience like? I bet you were nervous, because you didn't know how to drive. But your driving instructor probably showed you how to drive with more confidence. The same principle applies here: this book shows you the way to FREEDOM. It was written to help you understand the concept of the Aloepreneur Lifestyle and to raise your awareness about an opportunity that can change your life. I hope that answers your question.

Me: This sounds really interesting! I'll definitely read it.

Yara: Okay. Thank you for your interest in *"The Aloepreneur Lifestyle"*. Do you have any other questions?

Me: No, thanks! I will contact you if I have any questions.

Yara: Please! Feel free to contact us if you have any further questions or concerns. Thanks for your time and have a good rest of the day!

Me: Thank you. You too - Bye!

It's no accident that you're reading this book right now. Whether you bought for yourself or someone gave it to you, you probably want to do something special with your life. You may not want money, but the things that money can buy: maybe you and your family would like to visit the Eiffel Tower in Paris or you need to take a vacation to Bahamas and relax. Maybe you want a bigger house, a new car. You want to feel better and look better. Whatever your dreams can be, you're at the right address.

Have a good reading!

The Author

Introduction

Hi, my name is Yara Loua, I have some bad news and some good news. Before I share the news with you let me introduce myself to you. I was born and raised in Ivory Coast, West Africa. I went to college in Ghana and completed my graduate studies in India. I was blessed and very fortunate to be given the opportunity to immigrate to the US via the Diversity Visa Lottery Program organized by the Department of State.

I have always been fascinated by the US and the American way of life. Since the age of 11, my dream was to one day live in America. I used to watch American movies and see people having big houses, nice cars and living a happy life. So when I was given the opportunity to move here I couldn't afford to miss it. I left everything behind, my parents, my friends and my small business. I even sold everything I owned to afford the flight ticket.

Believe it or not after a week in the US I wanted to go back home; the reality was different to what I saw on movies. The situation didn't look good at all, far away from the American Dream I pictured in my mind. Since I couldn't go back home right away because my flight ticket was only a one-way ticket and I was broke, I had to find a way to make my dream come true. So I needed to look at things from a different perspective and focus on how to make things better. I realized that for things to get better I needed to make decisions and take massive actions.

I was opened to any ideas that could help me achieve my goals. I needed to move fast and learn more about the way things work in America; and the best place for me to start my journey and learn more about the American culture and its people was to join the military. The military has helped me to learn more about myself and others. It has given me the opportunity to develop new skills and master new ones such as patience, self-discipline, leadership, courage and many other skills important in life.

My hunger for success was immense, I wanted to try everything and I was always opened to new opportunities that came my way. Jumping from opportunities to opportunities and keeping on knocking on more doors, I finally found the right opportunity that would lead me to the American Dream and help me make a positive impact on the lives of others. I couldn't keep all this for me that is the reason I wrote this book to share it with you.

Coming back to our news, do you want to hear the good ones or the bad ones? Alright! Let's start first with the bad news. Some of the bad news I want to share with you are about things you already know. You may be living that situation or someone else you know is presently living it.

According to the US Department of Agriculture (USDA), there were over 46 million Americans living on food stamp in 2014. For our non-American audience who don't know about food stamp, it is a program that help low-income individual or family to afford food every month. Food stamp beneficiaries represent almost 15% of the US population and this tells me that those people earn less than $1,265 a month as a single person or earn less than $2,584 a month as a family of four in order to qualify for the program. And we taxpayers have to spend over $5.9 billion a month to take care of food stamp people. There is nothing wrong on helping people for food. But won't it be better to help those people take care of themselves and be independent? Can we understand that it is better to teach a man to fish than to give him a fish?

Another issue is the national student loan debt which is over $1.2 trillion. According to a recent article on the CNN website, there are over 40 million Americans with student debt. On average, students can expect to spend a national estimate of approximately $22,000 per year on an undergraduate post-secondary education. If the student is in school for four year to complete a degree, the total cost will be around $88,000. If the entire amount is financed in loans at a fixed rate of 5.75 percent, the total cost of the loan would average out to approximately $147,000. Most American will be paying this loan for their entire life. Unfortunately this loan cannot be forgiven even if you file for bankruptcy. Let's move on!

About 40 percent of American children under the age of 5 spend at least part of their week in the care of somebody other than a parent. Child care in the US can cost anywhere from $4,000 to $15,000 per year, depending on the region and quality of care. But Jonathan Cohn, an American author and journalist who writes mainly on United States public policy and political issues, said "trusting your child with someone else is one of the hardest things a parent has to do – and in the US, it's harder still, because American day care is a mess." Another reality is that family doesn't spend time anymore. According to a recent study, the average time a father spend with his children is 7 minutes a day and 21 minutes a day with his wife.

Last but not least, the problem of healthcare. According to a recent study by the Nerd Wallet Health, a division of the price comparison website, "Bankruptcies resulting from unpaid medical bills will affect nearly 2 million people this year—making health care the No. 1 cause of such filings, and outpacing bankruptcies due to credit-card bills or unpaid mortgages, according to new data. And even having health insurance doesn't buffer consumers against financial hardship."

Now, let me share this with you before we jump to our good news. Most people I met was complaining about their current situations. They were finding themselves squeezed financially at the end of every month. Instead of having extra money with which to enjoy the American Dream, they were experiencing the American Nightmare of working too hard but never having quite enough. I was surprised to see my brothers and sisters from Africa with two or three jobs working so hard for little. I felt sorry for them because they were **underpaid and overworked.**

In the other hand, people who were making more money couldn't have time to enjoy with their love ones. Even if they made six figures a year as a corporate employee or self-employed, they couldn't have total control of their time and spend quality time with their family because they were busy with work and had to meet deadlines they couldn't afford to miss. Their family may have all the luxury in the world but suffer from their absence. Such parents can't even attend their kids' school events, birthday parties, or share a family dinner with them. They are always on the run and when they come home from work every day they are tired or they have to continue at home the work they couldn't complete at work. Basically they earn lot of money but no time to enjoy life outside of work. They are known as the **overpaid and dissatisfied.**

Another issue is the problem of unemployment. According to a recent article on the CNBC website, 40 percent of the 8.5 million unemployed Americans have quit looking for jobs. Some of the reasons include a tight jobs market, the skills gap between what employers want and what prospective employees have to offer, and a benefits program that, while reduced from its recession level, still remains helpful have combined to keep workers on the sidelines.

Listen! The list may go on and on but I won't waste your time with bad news as the news media do. I am here to bring you hope and share with you a better way to achieve your dreams. Are you ready to hear the good news?

The good news I want to share with you may work for you or not, I don't need you to believe me because everyone's experience is different. The evidence is that students from the same school, having the same courses, are likely to have different results at the end of the final examination. Some will get 'A', 'B', 'C' or fail and get an 'F', this is called life and this is the only explanation I can give you for now. But what is very important is to have a look and an open mind about the information I am about to share. Folks, there is hope and the American Dream is still possible!

Today, you can take control of your destiny only if you are willing to learn. I can guarantee you it is achievable because thousands of people have already used the same principles taught in this book to achieve their dreams.

How would you feel, if you drive a powerful and brand-new car? Assuming this car is an SUV and you know this is the right vehicle to take you to your final destination. I bet you will be happy and have peace of mind because you know, no matter the number of stops you can make on your way, no matter how bad is the weather, no matter what time of day you're driving, you will reach your destination. This is exactly how I feel every day with what I am about to share with you.

Moreover, I've learnt over the past three years I've spent in the US, to become successful you need to develop collaborative, achievement-driven, supportive relationships with people who share the same goals with you. You can only achieve success if you create a win-win situation for everyone.

As Karl Marx said "Experience praises the most happy the one who made the most people happy." If I am happy today, I want you to be happy too.

I've discovered the vehicle that will take each of us to our final destination. This vehicle is not perfect but better, anyone regardless of ethnicity, gender, religion, sexuality, political affiliation, age, or disability can afford to drive and reach their final destination.

I have personally called this vehicle the "Aloepreneur Lifestyle"

Today you can achieve your dreams and leave a more promising future to your community. You can now take control of your own destiny and never rely again on the economy, the government, your job, your boss, or anyone else. Are you ready to learn more about this lifestyle?

Let's start the show!

The Aloepreneur Lifestyle Revealed

Who are the Aloepreneurs?

They are people just like you and I who **use Aloe every day** to improve their **health** and **wealth**. Their mission is to educate and encourage the use of Aloe in every household in their community and increase people awareness about owning their own Aloe business. The Aloepreneurs have established a lifelong partnership with the World Leader of Aloe to achieve their dreams and leave a more promising future to their community.

"How would you feel if you don't have to worry about money, health, and time anymore? Won't you be the happiest person on earth?"

When you look better, feel better and fall in love with a certain lifestyle, you can only share your story with others. How would you feel if you don't have to worry about money, health, and time anymore? Won't you be the happiest person on earth?

If you are reading this book today, chances are, you are currently not living the Aloepreneur Lifestyle or in other word you are not using the Aloe formula – a formula that comprises three essential life components which are **more money** in your bank account; **more time** for yourself, your family, and your community; and finally a **better health**. Most people I know have one or two but not all the three.

The Aloe Formula

ALOE = MONEY + TIME + HEALTH

You don't have to believe me but I need you to have an open mind about what we're going to discuss in the next chapters. As Frank Zappa said: "A mind is like a parachute. It doesn't work if it is not open." Hopefully, we agree not to behave like people at the time of Galileo who called him a liar when he said "the Earth was moving around the Sun". Therefore, if I tell you there is a unique opportunity that can make you retire in less than five years and make your family never work again for money, could you promise me not to call it a SCAM or a PYRAMID SCHEME?

If your answer is "yes". Please continue with your reading.

Thank you for giving me the trust and latitude to share my experience with you. I can guarantee you if this opportunity was illegal I would have been the first to be in jail; so you don't have to worry!

Most people was introduced to the Aloepreneur Lifestyle from a relative, a friend, a coworker, an acquaintance or a post from social media. As for me, it was my mother who introduced me to this unique lifestyle and I will always be grateful for her for everything she has given me and most importantly done for me.

If you also received this book from someone else, chances are, that person is presently transitioning from his or her current lifestyle to the Aloepreneur Lifestyle and wants you to take advantage of the same opportunity. As a common courtesy, don't forget to call back that person and say "Thank you!" because you won't be the same after reading the next chapters.

You have probably heard the word opportunity or read something about it, "Nothing is more expensive than a missed opportunity. It comes like a snail, and once it has passed you it changes into a rabbit and is gone." I don't think you can afford missing this opportunity because you deserve so much better in your life and we all do!

Today, you can choose to live the Aloepreneur Lifestyle and enjoy the possibility to work for yourself, to wake up with a new outlook on your life, to be there to see your kids grow up, to have time to spend with your family, to have the time and money to take vacations, and to make real plans for the future. You may be telling yourself, "This sounds too good to be true. Why I never heard about such lifestyle on TV or Radio?" That's right!

Such lifestyle can never be advertised on Public Television or Radio because if it's advertised there would be no reason for you to work again for someone else. Do you know the number of people who hate their jobs? According to the 2013 Gallup Poll, "70 percent of Americans hate their jobs". And if nobody wants a job, this could be a big problem for Uncle Sam and your Boss. Do you know that workers pay more taxes to Uncle Sam than Business Owners and Employees produce more money to their Bosses or Employers?

This could lead to the collapse of our current economic system if everyone becomes his or her own boss. It's similar to the image of everyone withdrawing their money from banks, just imagine how this could be a disaster for banks. So don't expect the media to educate you about that. On the contrary, they will use "fear of loss" tactics to keep you stick to your job or they will discourage you to take any initiative in becoming your own boss. You may hear things like: "The economy is bad", " Going into business for yourself is risky", "Oh! this is a pyramid scheme", " If you quit your job, how are you going to pay for your family healthcare?", " If you quit this job, you won't find any better", etc.

Please don't listen to such comments, because if you do so you would be allowing them to make decisions for you instead of making your own decisions. They will run your life, control you and make you live the life they think you should have. Our main goal is to educate you about the concept of the Aloepreneur Lifestyle and give you the opportunity to make your own decisions. So what's the Aloepreneur Lifestyle?

The Aloepreneur Lifestyle – a new way of life that provides you with more and better opportunities to improve your health and wealth using the miraculous plant of Aloe.

We have been coaching and helping thousands of people start their Aloe business from home. When I started my Aloe Business, I've never imagined working full-time somewhere else and being able to run a part-time business that operates in over 160 countries. This opportunity has helped thousands of people across the globe to have total control of their lives. They have built their business around their families, interests and achieved their desired lifestyle. What you are going to discover in the next chapters is based on a proven system that is so simple anyone can do it. Again, this opportunity has already helped millions of people across the globe to run a successful global business and make their dream come true.

Our goal is to inform and educate you about the Aloepreneur Lifestyle so that you can make more informed decisions. You are going to learn how to improve your health and build your wealth on your own pace.

SECTION ONE

IMPROVING YOUR HEALTH

The Aloepreneur Lifestyle also means living a happy and healthy lifestyle. We have our own way to define quality of life. For the Aloepreneurs, quality of life means being able to sleep at night, walk without pain, eat and enjoy food, have a working memory, and achieve things in your life that mean something to you. A healthy lifestyle means time with family, a walk in the woods, a positive mental outlook and an ability to handle stress without flipping out. It also means treating your body with respect and experiencing the joy of feeling it work well in return. And finally, a healthy lifestyle means vibrant energy, daily optimism and even good sexual energy. This section features the Aloepreneurs' healthy lifestyle. You will learn more about the benefits of Aloe and other useful tips to fully enjoy this new lifestyle.

Chapter 1. The hidden secrets of Aloe

1. If a plant were a pharmacy it should be called Aloe

The Aloe or **Aloe Vera** is one of the world's most powerful medicinal plants and is full of nutritional benefits. It contains over 200 active components including vitamins, minerals, amino acids, enzymes, polysaccharide, and fatty acids – no wonder it's used for such a wide range of remedies! It is a succulent plant and part of the lily family (Liliaceae), the same family that garlic and onions belong to. Different parts of the plant are used for different purposes and Aloe Vera has both internal and external applications.

There are over 400 species of Aloe, with Aloe Vera one of the best known. The name Aloe Vera derives from the Arabic word "Alloeh" meaning "shining bitter substance," while "Vera" in Latin means "true." The scientific name of the Aloe Vera is the Aloe Barbadensis Miller. 2000 years ago, the Greek scientists regarded Aloe Vera as the **universal panacea**. The Egyptians called Aloe **"the plant of immortality."**

Did you know that the "Wise King" and many other historical leaders depended on the benefits of Aloe?

The Aloe plant has been known and used for centuries for its health, beauty, medicinal and skin care properties. It has been used for medicinal purposes in several cultures for millennia: Greece, Egypt, India, Mexico, Japan and China.

The "Wise King" and many other historical leaders depended on the benefits of Aloe Vera. Egyptian queens Nefertiti and Cleopatra used it as part of their regular beauty regimes. Alexander the Great, and Christopher Columbus used it to treat soldiers' wounds. King Solomon grow his own Aloe, Mahatma Ghandi used it to stay alive.

Did you know that Aloe is mentioned in the Holy Bible at least 6 different places?

The Bible mentions 128 plants that were part of everyday life in ancient Israel and its Mediterranean neighbors. One of those plants is the Aloe and it has been mentioned at 6 different places: **John 19:39-40; Numbers 24:6; Psalms 45:8; Proverbs 7:17; Solomon 4:14; John 19:39.**

I personally think Aloe is a plant of God, therefore a blessed plant.

Did you know that Aloe Vera is the only known natural source of vitamin B12?

Aloe Vera is the only known natural source of vitamin B12. B12 supports proper function of the nervous system, brain and the production of blood. In other words, it keeps your nerves and red blood cells healthy. A deficiency in vitamin B12 can result in a host of illness like anemia, fatigue, weakness, constipation, loss of appetite, weight loss, depression, poor memory, soreness of the mouth, asthma, vision problems, and a low sperm count. If you know you are a heavy drinker and smoker, a strict vegetarian, pregnant and breast-feeding, or an elderly you may require vitamin B12 supplements or drink Aloe on a daily basis.

2. The Power of Aloe

Why Aloepreneurs stay healthy? You should already know the answer by now, because we consume Aloe every single day. Aloe is part of the diet of all Aloepreneurs and this is not a secret. But, I want to share with you the point of view of a British expert – Dr. Peter Atherton.

Dr. Peter Atherton is regarded as one of the world's experts in the field of Aloe Vera's medical properties. He developed an interest in complementary medicine after his 30 year career in general medicinal practice. In order to test the validity of the medical properties that have been traditionally ascribed to Aloe Vera, Dr. Atherton started a two year research fellowship at Oxford University studying the medicinal effects of Aloe Vera. What he found from the research provided him enough confidence that he began limited clinical trials in his own practice, and the results were very encouraging. Below, he shares with us his top 10 reasons to drink Aloe Vera Gel from our Aloe Store.

Top 10 Benefits & Medicinal Uses For Aloe Vera

1. A general tonic for good health

By drinking the Aloe gel with all its important ingredients including 19 of the 20 amino acids needed by the human body, and seven of the eight essential ones that just cannot be made, the body is able to get enough to allow complex enzyme systems to work really well. This means the body can function at 100%. The net result to the individual is a wonderful feeling of wellbeing which tends to go with an improved ability to withstand and even fight illness.

2. A useful source of vitamins

Aloe Vera Gel contains a large range of vitamins – even trace elements of vitamin B12 which is rarely found in plants. Apart from vitamin A, it contains B-group vitamins, vitamin C, vitamin E and folic acid. Many of these vitamins cannot be stored by the body so we need to constantly top them up from the food that we eat. What better way than by drinking a daily amount of Aloe gel while at the same time building up a body's defense system against oxidative stress naturally?

3. A useful source of minerals

Some of the minerals found in Aloe Vera include calcium, sodium, potassium, iron, chromium, magnesium, manganese, copper and zinc. This is because the plant tends to grow in areas where soils are rich in these minerals and its roots are able to absorb them and deliver them to us in a very available form.

4. Anti-inflammatory and pain killing effect

Among the substances that have been identified in Aloe Vera are several that are anti-inflammatory and pain killing which are very helpful for people experiencing these symptoms.

5. Antiviral activity

Within the mucilage layer of the leaf which surrounds the inner gel there is a long chain sugar or polysaccharide. This has the capability of being able to help defend us against attacks by various viruses from the simple ones causing every day illnesses to the more complex ones. This sugar has actually been extracted from Aloe Vera in the USA and made into a drug but it is actually not necessary to extract the magic bullet. Drinking the Gel is just as effective.

6. Increases the activity of fibroblasts

Fibroblasts are specialized cells found in the skin and their job is to produce fiber such as collagen and elastin. These fibers give the skin its structure and, of course, make it look plump and elastic. This is fine from a cosmetic point of view but they are also extremely important in wound healing, as these fibers create a mesh or network over which the new skin cells advance to close the wound. The effect of Aloe Vera is to stimulate them to reproduce faster and therefore, being more of them, they make more fiber. The time taken for wounds to heal under the influence of Aloe Vera can be reduced by up to a third.

7. Effect on the skin

When they are first produced deep in the epidermis, skin cells are rather large and very much alive, but by the time they reach the surface after 21–28 days (in normal skin) they are a shadow of their former selves and are transformed into just thin flakes of keratin which eventually fall off. Aloe Vera Gel provides the essential nutrition to feed the basal cells and therefore the skin remains healthy and is able to perform its vital functions more efficiently – as well as looking much better!

8. Effects on gut flora

Aloe Vera is a natural balancer in many areas and nowhere more so than inside the gut where it tends to regulate the proportion of bacteria and yeasts that inhabit it. At various times in life people can develop an imbalance through a variety of causes which can lead to problems and, as with probiotics, Aloe may often help to normalize the situation.

9. Assists in healthy digestion

A healthy digestive tract ensures that nutrients from the food we eat are absorbed into the bloodstream. There is clear, clinical evidence that by drinking

Aloe Vera Gel the bowel is able to absorb these nutrients more efficiently, especially protein. I also suspect that many other substances are much better absorbed under its influence.

10. Effect on the gut

Aloe Vera has a wonderfully beneficial action on bowel function which results in a smooth and efficient transit of contents, often eradicating inconvenient, colicky pain.

Should I grow my own Aloe?

It is possible to grow your own Aloe but we do not recommend it. One of the reason is that Aloe likes sun and cannot grow in all areas of the world because of the different climate zones. It cannot withstand chilling temperatures and require full sun for at least six hours per day but best growth is found where the plant receives at least eight hours of bright light. For someone living in Alaska it will be harder to grow such a plant and even if you grow it indoors, you CANNOT guarantee its potency or best quality. If you plan consuming it, be forewarned that your indoor Aloe plant may contain some aloin (a compound found in the skin which can have a laxative effect.) and can only be conserved in the fridge for about a week. You don't want that! You want to make sure you have sufficient Aloe Vera Gel for your daily personal consumption.

However, It is important to know that a fruit or vegetable when cut and in contact with air, also begins to oxidize earlier to darken and lose its virtues. This is also the case of the Aloe Vera Gel which in contact with air loses all his qualities and I don't think you want to consume a product that has lost its vitamins and enzymes. I remembered a friend of mine who used to live in California, when he moved to Tennessee he came with his Aloe plant but unfortunately the plant died.

Purchasing Aloe: Choose the right Aloe for your needs

Where to buy pure Aloe Vera Gel? Should I go to Walmart, Kmart or any retail stores?

This a great question! You need to choose your Aloe products carefully. According to ConsumerLab.com, 50% of the Aloe products available on the markets had little or no Aloe including one Aloe Pill and one Aloe Gel. In addition, many companies buy Aloe as a commodity, looking for the lowest price without regard for where and how it was grown.

Aloe grows in dry climates and absorbs available water to survive in dry spells. As a result, pesticides, herbicides, fungicides and fertilizers present in ground water are also readily absorbed and stored in the Aloe leaf.

For safety and purity, consider only an Aloe brand independently certified by the International Aloe Science Council (IASC).

Coming back to our questions, you won't find the Aloe used by Aloepreneurs in stores like Walmart, Kmart, or any retail stores. We recommend you to purchase your Aloe with an Aloepreneur and chances are the person who gave you this book has an Aloe Store. Thanks to our partner

(The World Leader of Aloe), we are able to consume top-quality Aloe products which are certified by the IASC.

Our Aloe products are available in over 160 countries and can be purchase with any Aloepreneur. Don't even bother looking elsewhere because you won't find a better product than our Aloe products!

Chapter 2. The World Leader of Aloe

1. <u>Products certified by IASC</u>

There are many companies out there that pretend to sell Aloe Vera, but we the Aloepreneurs have chosen the World Leader of Aloe not because they are the world number one, but because they produce the finest Aloe Vera products in the world. They own all the Aloe plantations used to make the products we consume, so they can guarantee the purity and potency of all the products.

In addition, the **World Leader of Aloe was the first company to be awarded the International Aloe Science Council's Seal of Approval.** They insist on the best and that's exactly what we get. The largest Aloe Vera plantation in the world is located in the Dominican Republic and have 30 million plants and harvest over 1 million pounds of Aloe per week.

Why the World Leader of Aloe?

- *World's No.1 grower of Aloe,*
- *No insecticides, pesticides or fertilizers,*
- *Hand harvested, hand filleted inner leaf gel,*
- *Patented stabilization process,*
- *Superior quality product.*
- *Certified by IFANCA as halal products*
- *Certified by Kosher rating*
- *Cruelty free and products not tested on animals*

The company has also another plantation in Texas; both the Texas and Dominican Republic farms use free range goats and sheep to naturally control weeds and provide 100% natural fertilizer. This allows to grow a superb crop without compromising the health of the Aloe or the environment. From planting to tending to harvesting, their Aloe plants are carefully nurtured with the same level of care and standards that they put into to every one of their final products. Their farmers harvest the Aloe by hand, treating it with great care. The leaves are processed within hours, so we get the purest, freshest Aloe Vera Gel intact with all its inherent qualities.

A tour in a world-class manufacturing plant

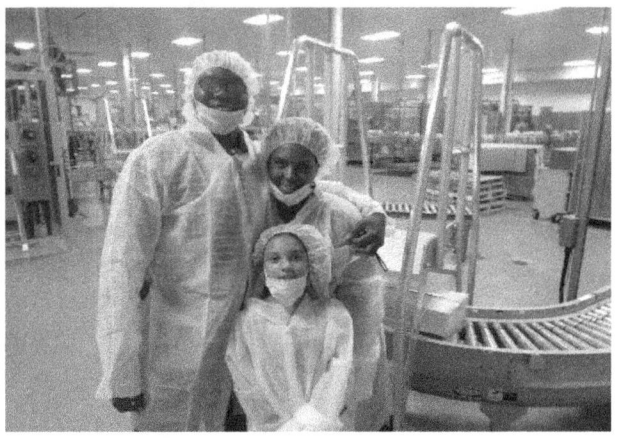

I personally visited with my family the facility where the Aloe products are manufactured and I can tell you this is an incredible manufacturing facility with the latest technologies you can imagine to guarantee you excellent Aloe products. To learn more about the World Leader of Aloe, contact the person who gave you this book or send us an email at info@aloepreneur.com and we will be happy to provide you with more information.

Chapter 3. Promoting healthy habits

1. <u>Healthy habits to improve your life</u>

Would you trade your health with a million dollars? I bet you will say "No!", even if I double the amount because you know your health is priceless. There is no need to have a million dollars if you are locked in the hospital, and money can't replace your health; that is why you have to take good care of yourself. As we all know, to improve the quality of our life we have to make good choices; so that we can feel better mentally and physically. Good choices or habits promote longevity and some of those habits include:

If you smoke, quit: Smoking leads to disease and disability and harms nearly every organ of the body. More than 16 million Americans are living with a disease caused by smoking. For every person who dies because of smoking, at least 30 people live with a serious smoking-related illness. Smoking causes cancer, heart disease, stroke, lung diseases, diabetes, and chronic obstructive pulmonary disease (COPD), which includes emphysema and chronic bronchitis. Smoking also increases risk for tuberculosis, certain eye diseases, and problems of the immune system, including rheumatoid arthritis. Smoking is a known cause of erectile dysfunction in males. Worldwide, tobacco use causes nearly 6 million deaths per year, and current trends show that tobacco use will cause more than 8 million deaths annually by 2030. Cigarette smoking is responsible for more than 480,000 deaths per year in the United States, including nearly 42,000 deaths resulting from secondhand smoke exposure. This is about one in five deaths annually, or 1,300 deaths every day. On average, smokers die 10 years earlier than nonsmokers. If smoking continues at the current rate among U.S. youth, 5.6 million of today's Americans younger than 18 years of age are expected to die prematurely from a smoking-related illness. This represents about one in every 13 Americans aged 17 years or younger who are alive today.

Eat a varied low-fat diet – Experts recommend five or more servings of fruits and vegetables each day, plenty of whole grains (which are high in dietary fiber as well as vitamins and minerals), and low-fat dairy products (for bone-strengthening calcium).

If you drink alcohol, quit: Excessive consumption of alcohol can lead to high blood pressure, heart disease (number one cause of death in America), cancer (number two cause of death in America), and other health problems.

Exercise regularly – Studies show that even 30 minutes of walking, swimming, playing golf, or other forms of exercise can help lower your risk of disease or premature death. But how many people exercise today with their busy schedules. Even walking simply becomes a problem because most people have a car or use the public transportation.

Avoid becoming seriously overweight: if you have two or three jobs, I don't think that you have time to cook for yourself. You will rather eat fast food or probably eat outside. If you live in the US, obesity is not something new to you even though America has lost is No.1 position. Mexico only two years ago unseated America as the fattest country in the world according to the World Health Organization (WHO). A recent study from Harvard's School of Public Health estimates obesity may account for as much as $190 billion annually or 21 percent of all US medical expenses. According to the American Heart Association, one in three US children are now considered overweight or obese. Obesity is linked to rising US rates of chronic illnesses and conditions, including diabetes, heart disease and cancer. Keep your weight in check by watching your calories and exercising.

Protect yourself from the sun – Too much sun damages your skin, promoting skin cancer and cataracts. Good reason for you to apply Aloe Vera on your skin. Use sunscreen, avoid long exposure, wear sunglasses, and examine your skin for irregularities.

Control stress – Stress substantially slows human body's ability to heal. A recent study showed that the stress a typical married couple feels during an ordinary half-hour argument is enough to slow their bodies' ability to heal from wounds by at least one day. You can't avoid stress but you can reduce it by exercising, meditating and pursuing other activities you enjoy.

Keep your hand clean – whether you use a hand sanitizer or wash your hand with soap, don't forget to clean your hand before, during, and after preparing food; before eating food; before and after caring for someone who is sick; before and after treating a cut or wound; after using the toilet; after changing diapers or cleaning up a child who has used the toilet; after blowing your nose, coughing, or sneezing; after touching an animal, animal feed, or animal waste; after handling pet food or pet treats; after touching garbage.

Chapter 4. Uses of dietary supplements

1. The reality is quite the opposite

You don't have to be rich to live healthy or be a physician to know that a healthy lifestyle will include both a balanced diet and exercise. But the question is - **How many people use organic food today? Eat five daily servings of fresh fruits and vegetables? Or walk at least 30 min a day?**

The reality is quite the opposite. Statistics show that only **9 percent of Americans eat five daily servings of fresh fruits and vegetables** – the amount recommended for obtaining the minimum level of nutrients believed necessary to prevent illness. **Only 20.8 percent of Americans engage in a physical activity program that is deemed consistent and worthy of health improvements**. One out of four Americans eats fast food every day. **Americans spend nearly $100 billion on fast food every year;** this amount of money is enough to stop world hunger for many years. It's not a surprise that **61 percent of the food Americans buy is highly processed.**

Nowadays, people don't feel like cooking at all. When they come home from work they are tired and they are looking for food they can put in a microwave and have dinner.

Some prefer to stop by the fast food restaurant and grab something to eat for the family. Eating fresh foods is no longer part of our habits because we have replaced it now with the packaged foods.

There is no secret why our great-great grandparents were living longer and healthier than our current generation because they were eating real food. Food came straight from farms and because food preservatives were not widely used yet, food was fresh. Because of the lack of processed food (food was not yet treated with additives, antibiotics and hormones to help preserve shelf life), their diets were nutrient dense allowing them to get the nutrition they needed from their food.

They didn't go to the doctor when they felt sick or take prescription medications. Doctor visits were saved for accidental injuries and life threatening illness. Can you believed that 70 percent of Americans take prescription drugs today? According to a recent study from Rochester Minnesota researchers, 70 percent of Americans are on at least one prescription drug, and more than half receive at least two prescriptions. Most common prescription drugs include antibiotics, antidepressants and painkillers opioids. Expenditures on prescription drugs reached $250 billion in 2009.

I remember when I came here three years ago I was 170 pounds, it took me less than a year to jump to 240 pounds. I realized that if I don't take control of my diet and exercise more I may end up in the hospital. Thanks to my Mother who recommended me Aloe, I started drinking Aloe Vera Gel to detoxify my body from all those toxins and supplement my diet.

The food we eat can affect our health and our risk for certain diseases. Ayurvedic physicians believed that: "**If your food is not good, your medicine has no effect. If your food is good, you do not need medicine.**" In addition, The founder of medicine, Hippocrates said: "**Let food be thy medicine and medicine be thy food**" . Therefore, it is significant to have a balanced diet. A balanced diet is one that gives your body the nutrition it needs to function properly. However, what are your options if you can't eat healthy? The solution is to supplement the food you eat with dietary supplements.

2. <u>Dietary Supplements: The solution for poor diet</u>

If you know, you are not exercising, consuming fruits, vegetables and organic foods regularly, it's time to consider dietary supplements. Dietary supplements, according to the definition given on the US Food and Drug Administration (FDA) website: *"Congress defined the term "dietary supplement" in the Dietary Supplement Health and Education Act (DSHEA) of 1994. A dietary supplement is a product taken by mouth that contains a "dietary ingredient" intended to supplement the diet. The "dietary ingredients" in these products may include: vitamins, minerals, herbs or other botanicals, amino acids, and substances such as enzymes, organ tissues, glandulars, and metabolites. Dietary supplements can also be extracts or concentrates, and may be found in many forms such as tablets, capsules, softgels, gelcaps, liquids, or powders. They can also be in other forms, such as a bar, but if they are, information on their label must not represent the product as a conventional food or a sole item of a meal or diet. Whatever their form may be, DSHEA places dietary supplements in a special category under the general umbrella of "foods," not drugs, and requires that every supplement be labeled a dietary supplement."*

3. <u>Doctors and nurses rely on supplements to stay healthy</u>

Even Doctors and nurses who practice conventional medicine may be skeptical about alternative therapies, but many use vitamin and mineral supplements themselves. In a survey of 181 cardiologists, nearly half were regularly taking antioxidant vitamins, including vitamin C and vitamin E, which are linked to the prevention of cancer and heart disease. A somewhat smaller percentage of the physicians (37 percent) recommended antioxidants routinely to their patients. Another survey of 665 dietitians in Washington State found that nearly 60 percent of them took some kind of nutritional supplement, either daily or occasionally.

Why Antioxidants are so important?

If you smoke or drink alcohol regularly, or you are often experiencing stress, you will like this section. Antioxidants are substances that may protect your cells against the effects of free radicals. Free radicals are molecules produced when your body breaks down food or is exposed to tobacco smoke, alcohol, pollutants such as nitrogen oxide and ozone, and ultraviolet light and other forms of radiation, including X rays. Free radicals may play a role in heart disease, cancer and other diseases.

How to stay healthy when you have limited resources?

Today, you can stay healthy when you have limited resources and this is possible thanks to supplements. Supplements are easy to obtain and less expensive than prescription drugs. But before taking any supplements it is important to talk with your family physician to know if it is right for your current situation. For example, if you are pregnant, nursing a baby, or have a chronic medical condition, such as, diabetes, hypertension or heart disease, be sure to consult your doctor or pharmacist before purchasing or taking any supplement. In most cases, your doctors shouldn't find any problem for you using supplements because physicians are good consumers of supplements themselves.

Why a dietary supplement is not a prescription drug?

Dietary supplements are products intended to supplement the diet and doesn't require a prescription. The Dietary Supplement Health and Education Act defines dietary supplements as a category of food. In addition, the FDA must approve any new drug before it can be legally sold in the US and dietary supplements don't need FDA approval. Dietary supplement manufacturers and distributors are not required to obtain approval from FDA before marketing dietary supplements.

This is why some supplements have a disclaimer that says: **"This statement has not been evaluated by the FDA. This product is not intended to diagnose, treat, cure, or prevent any disease"**

In addition, this statement or "disclaimer" is required by law (DSHEA) when a manufacturer makes a structure/function claim on a dietary supplement label. In general, these claims describe the role of a nutrient or dietary ingredient intended to affect the structure or function of the body. The manufacturer is responsible for ensuring the accuracy and truthfulness of these claims; they are not approved by FDA. For this reason, the law says that if a dietary supplement label includes such a claim, it must state in a "disclaimer" that FDA has not evaluated this claim. The disclaimer must also state that this product is not intended to "diagnose, treat, cure or prevent any disease," because only a drug can legally make such a claim.

Popular supplements and their common uses

Again, I am NOT a licensed medical doctor and makes no claims to be. The list discussed are not intended to diagnose, mitigate, treat, cure or prevent a specific disease or class of diseases. You should consult your family physician if you are experiencing a medical problem.

Acidophilus – Chronic gastrointestinal tract disorders (such as irritable bowel syndrome, recurrent gas and bloating, and inflammatory bowel disease) and vaginal yeast infections.

Aloe vera – Applied externally: minor burns including sunburn, cuts and abrasions, insect bites and stings, welts, small skin ulcers, and frostbite. It also relieves the itch of shingles including herpes zoster, and may help clear up warts. Applied internally: soothes ulcers, heartburn, and other digestive complaints.

Alpha-lipoic acid – Numbness, tingling, and other symptoms of nerve damage in people with diabetes or other conditions. It also protects the liver in hepatitis, alcohol abuse, or exposure to poisons or toxic chemicals. It aids in preventing cataracts; it may help preserve memory in Alzheimer's disease. It serves as a high-potency antioxidant and possible immune booster, combating a wide range of disorders, including psoriasis, fibromyalgia, and AIDS.

Amino acids (glycine, alanine, proline, valine, leucine, isoleucine, methionine, phenylalanine, tyrosine, tryptophan, serine, threonine, cysteine, asparagine, glutamine, lysine, arginine, histidine, aspartate, glutamate) – heart disease, lower blood pressure, and boost immune function, improve some nerve disorders.

Astragalus – enhances immunity, helps fight respiratory infections, and bolsters the immune system in people undergoing cancer treatment.

Bee products (bee pollen, propolis, and royal jelly) – may help hay fever symptoms, aids in healing skin abrasions.

Beta-carotene – acts as a preventive for cancer and heart disease, may reverse some precancerous conditions, has cell-protesting properties that may aid in the treatment of a wide variety of ailments from Alzheimer's to male infertility.

Bilberry – maintains healthy vision and improves night vision and poor visual adaptation to bright light; a wide array of eye disorders including diabetic retinopathy, cataracts, and macular degeneration; relieves varicose veins and hemorrhoids, especially in pregnancy.

Biotin – promotes healthy nails and hair; helps the body use carbohydrates, fats, and protein; may improve blood sugar control in people with diabetes.

Black cohosh – reduces menopausal symptoms, particularly hot flashes; eases menstrual pain and other difficulties, such as PMS; works as an anti-inflammatory; relieves muscle pain; helps clear mucous membranes and relieve coughs.

Calcium – maintains bones and teeth, helps prevent progressive bone loss and osteoporosis; aids heart and muscle contraction, nerves impulses, and blood clotting;

may help lower blood pressure in people with hypertension; eases heartburn.

Carotenoids – may lower the risk of certain types of cancers, including prostate and lung cancer; may provide protection against heart disease; slow the development of macular degeneration; enhance immunity.

Cat's claw – may enhance immunity, making it useful for sinusitis and other infections; support cancer treatment; may help relieve chronic pain; reduces pain and inflammation from gout or arthritis.

Cayenne – Applied externally: relieves arthritis pain; reduce nerve pain of shingles, diabetes, surgery, or tic douloureux. Applied internally: alleviate indigestion.

Chamomile – promotes general relaxation and relieves anxiety; alleviates insomnia; heals mouth sores and treats gum disease; soothes skin rashes and burns, including sunburn; relieves red and irritated eyes; eases menstrual cramps; treats bowel inflammation, digestive upset, and heartburn.

Chasteberry (vitex) – alleviates symptoms of Premenstrual Syndrome (PMS); regulates menstruation, promotes fertility; eases menopausal hot flashes.

Chromium – essential for the breakdown of protein, fat, and carbohydrates; helps the body maintain normal blood sugar (glucose) levels; may lower total blood cholesterol, LDL or bad cholesterol, and triglyceride levels; may enhance weight-loss efforts.

Coenzyme Q10 – improves the heart and circulation in those with congestive heart failure, a weakened heart muscle, high blood pressure, heart rhythm disorders, chest pain or angina; maintains healthy gums and teeth; protects the nerves and may help slow Alzheimer's or Parkinson's disease; may help prevent cancer and heart disease, and play a role in slowing down age-related degenerative changes; may improve the course of AIDS or cancer.

Copper – strengthens blood vessels, bones, tendons, and nerves; helps maintain fertility; ensures healthy hair and skin pigmentation; promotes blood clotting.

Cranberry – lower urinary tract infections or bladder infections; helps deodorize urine; and may prevent recurrence of cystitis or bladder infections.

Dandelion – Bolsters the liver; useful during cases of hepatitis or liver inflammation and jaundice; aids digestion by stimulating release of bile from the liver and gallbladder; may help prevent gallstones and endometriosis.

Dehydroepiandrosterone (DHEA) – may lower risk of heart disease; aids in glucose management in some people with diabetes; boosts the immune system; relieves some lupus symptoms; may help people with HIV/AIDS.

Dong quai – may help ease monthly menstrual cramps; may reduce hot flashes associated with menopause.

Echinacea – reduces the body's susceptibility to colds and flu; limits the duration and severity of infections; helps fight recurrent respiratory, middle ear, urinary tract, and vaginal yeast infections; speeds the healing of skin wounds and inflammations.

Ephedra – eases congestion, and labored breathing that are caused by allergies or asthma; relieves pressure and congestion in sinus infections or sinusitis; may aid weight loss.

Evening primrose oil – eases rheumatoid arthritis pain; can minimize symptoms of diabetic nerve damage; relieve eczema symptoms; helps treat premenstrual syndrome, endometriosis, and menstrual cramps; lessens inflammation of acne, rosacea, and muscle strains.

Feverfew (febrifuge) – helps prevent or reduce the intensity of migraines; may ease menstrual complaints.

Fish oils (omega-3) – helps prevent cardiovascular disease; useful for other circulatory conditions as well; block disease related-inflammatory responses in the body; may lower blood pressure.

5- Hydroxytryptophan (5-HTP) – relieves depression; helps overcome insomnia; aids in weight control; may ease pain of fibromyalgia; aids in migraines.

Flavonoids – reduce the risk of heart disease; may prevent breast, prostate, and other types of cancer; lessen the change of age-related vision problems, such as cataracts; minimize the symptoms of hay fever and asthma; fight viral infections.

Flaxseed oil – helps protect against cancer, heart disease, cataracts, and gallstones; reduces inflammation associated with gout and lupus; promotes healthy skin, hair, and nails; benefits acne, eczema, psoriasis, rosacea, and sunburn; may be useful for infertility, impotence, menstrual cramps, and endometriosis; aids in nerve disorders; relieves constipation, gallstones, and diverticular disorders.

Folic acid (Vitamin B9) – protects against birth defects; reduce heart disease and stroke risk; lower risk for several cancers.

Garcinia cambogia – may suppress appetite and aid dieting.

Garlic – may lower cholesterol levels; reduces blood clotting; fights infections; acts to boost immunity; may prevent some cancers; may produce a slight drop in blood pressure; combats fungal infections.

Ginger – alleviates nausea and dizziness; may relieve pain and inflammation of arthritis; eases muscle aches; relieves allergies; reduces flatulence.

Ginkgo biloba (Ginkgo) – slows the progression of Alzheimer's symptoms; sharpens memory and concentration, particularly in older people; lessens depression and anxiety in older people; alleviates coldness in the extremities (Raynaud's disease) and painful leg cramps or intermittent claudication; helps headaches, ringing in the ears or tinnitus, and dizziness; may restore erections in men with impotence.

Ginseng (Panax) – combats the physical effects of stress; aids in impotence and infertility in men; boosts energy.

Glucosamine – relieves pain, stiffness, and swelling of the knees, fingers, and other joints due to osteoarthritis or rheumatoid arthritis; helps reduce arthritis back and neck pain; may speed the healing of sprains and strengthen joints, preventing future injury.

Goldenseal – promotes healing of canker sores and cold sores; helps destroy the virus that causes warts; bolsters the immune system; calms a nauseated stomach; may help urinary tract infections; aids in eye infections.

Gotu kola – aids in burns and wounds; builds connective tissue; strengthen veins; improves memory.

Grape seed extract – blood vessel disorders; protects against vision damage; lessens the risk of heart disease and cancer; reduces the rate of collagen breakdown in the skin.

Green tea – may help prevent cancer; protect against heart disease; inhibits tooth decay; promotes longevity.

Gugulipid – helps lower high blood cholesterol and high blood triglycerides; reduces heart disease risk; arthritis inflammation; may aid weight loss.

Hawthorn – relieves chest pain of angina; lowers high blood pressure; helps the heart pump more efficiently in people with congestive heart failure; corrects irregular heartbeat or cardiac arrhythmia.

Iodine – corrects an iodine deficiency; ensures proper functioning of the thyroid gland; may help treat fibrocystic breasts.

Iron – aids in iron-deficiency anemia; often needed during pregnancy; by women with heavy menstrual periods.

Kava – combats anxiety; eases panic attacks; helps induce sleep; relieve pain.

Lecithin and Choline – helps in preventing gallstones; strengthen the liver, making them useful in the treatment of hepatitis and cirrhosis; aids the liver in ridding the body of toxins in patients undergoing chemotherapy for cancer; diminish heartburn symptoms; may boost memory and enhance brain function.

Licorice – reduces symptoms of chronic fatigue and fibromyalgia; helps digestive problems; helps treat eczema; promotes hepatitis recovery; enhance immunity; eases respiratory illnesses; may be useful for menstrual disorders and menopause.

Maca (Peruvian Ginseng, Lepidium mevenii) - used for anemia, Chronic Fatigue Syndrome (CFS), and enhancing energy, stamina, athletic performance, memory, and fertility. Used for weak bones, depression, to arouse sexual desire and to boost immune system.

Magnesium – helps protect against heart disease and irregular heartbeat; eases fibromyalgia symptoms; lowers high blood pressure; may reduce the severity of asthma attacks; improves symptoms of Premenstrual Syndrome (PMS); helps in preventing the complication of diabetes.

Melatonin – relieves insomnia; promote restful sleep, even during nighttime pain or stress-related sleep disturbances; diminishes the effects and shortens the course of jet lag.

Milk thistle – protects the liver from toxins, including drugs, poisons, and chemicals. Treats liver disorders, such as cirrhosis and hepatitis; reduces liver damage from excessive alcohol; aids in the treatment and prevention of gallstones; helps clear psoriasis.

Mushrooms – build immunity; help prevent cancer; enhance cancer treatments; alleviate bronchitis, sinusitis. Treat chronic fatigue syndrome; help prevent heart disease.

Nettle (urtica dioica) – helps body remove excess fluid; relieves allergy symptoms (hay fever); reduces inflammation; may ease prostate symptoms; and helps urinary tract infections.

Niacin (vitamin B3 or nicotinic acid) – lowers cholesterol; may improve circulation; may ease symptoms of arthritis; may relieve depression; may prevent progression of type 1 diabetes.

Pantothenic acid – promotes a healthy central nervous system; helps the body use carbohydrates, fats, and protein; may improve chronic fatigue syndrome, migraines, heartburn, and allergies.

Pau d'arco (Tabebuia impetiginosa) – treats vaginal yeast infections; helps get rid of warts; reduces inflammation of the airways in bronchitis; may be useful in treating such immune-related disorders as asthma, eczema, psoriasis, and bacterial and viral infections.

Peppermint (mentha piperita) – relieves heartburn, nausea, and indigestion. Eases symptoms of diverticulosis and irritable bowel syndrome; helps dissolve gallstones; sweetens the breath; soothe muscle aches; eases coughs and congestion due to allergies or colds.

Phosphorus – builds strong bones and maintains skeletal integrity; helps from tooth enamel and strengthens teeth.

Potassium – helps lower blood pressure; may prevent high blood pressure, heart disease, and stroke.

Psyllium – relieves constipation, diarrhea. Treats diverticular disease and irritable bowel syndrome; helps prevent gallstones; reduces hemorrhoid pain; may lower cholesterol; and facilitates weight loss.

Riboflavin – prevents or delays the onset of cataracts; reduces the frequency and severity of migraines; improves skin blemishes caused by rosacea.

Saw palmetto (serenoa repens) - eases frequent nighttime urination and other symptoms of an enlarged prostate; relieves prostate inflammation; may boost immunity and treat urinary tract infections.

Selenium – works with vitamin E to help prevent cancer and heart disease; protects against cataracts and macular degeneration; fights viral infections; reduces the severity of cold sores and shingles; may slow the progression of HIV/AIDS; and helps relieve lupus symptoms.

Shark cartilage – may help fight cancer; may ease arthritic joint pain, temper the skin lesions of psoriasis, and help heal cold sores.

Siberian ginseng (Eleutherococcus senticosus) – combats stress-related illness; fights fatigue; restore energy; enhances immunity and helps with chronic fatigue syndrome and fibromyalgia; supports sexual function; may improve fertility in both sexes; eases symptoms of menopause; and may boost mental alertness in people with Alzheimer's disease.

Soy isoflavones – reduce the frequency and severity of hot flashes and other menopausal symptoms; may protect against coronary heart disease; may forestall certain cancers; and may help prevent osteoporosis.

Spirulina and kelp – Spirulina treats bad breath, and adds protein, vitamins, and minerals to the diet. Kelp treats underactive thyroid and provides essential nutrients.

St. John's wort (hypericum perforatum) – treats depression; helps fight off viral and bacterial infections; may help treat premenstrual syndrome (PMS) and fibromyalgia; helps relieve chronic pain; soothes hemorrhoids; and may aid in weight loss.

Tea tree oil (Melaleuca alternifolia) – disinfects and promotes the healing of cuts and scrapes; minimize scarring; speeds recovery from bug or spider bites and stings (bee stings); and fights athlete's foot, fungal nail infections, and yeast infections.

Thiamin (vitamin B1) – aids energy production; promotes healthy nerves; may improve mood; strengthens the heart; and soothes heartburn.

Trace minerals (Boron, silicon, manganese, vanadium, molybdenum) – Boron and silicon aid in building strong bones, teeth, and nails. Manganese treats heart arrhythmias, osteoporosis, epileptic seizures, sprains, and back pain. Vanadium may aid people with diabetes. Molybdenum helps the body use iron.

Valerian (Valeriana officinalis) – promotes restful sleep; soothes stress and anxiety; improves the symptoms of some digestive disorders.

Vitamin A – fights colds, flu, and other types of infections; treats skin disorders; heals wounds, burns, and ulcers. Maintains eye health; enhances chemotherapy; eases inflammatory bowel disease.

Vitamin B6 – helps prevent cardiovascular disease and strokes; helps to lift depression; eases insomnia; treats carpal tunnel syndrome; may lessen PMS symptoms; and helps relieve asthma attacks.

Vitamin B12 – prevents a form of anemia; helps reduce depression; thwarts nerve pain, numbness, and tingling; lowers the risk of heart disease; may improve multiple sclerosis and tinnitus.

Vitamin C – enhances immunity; minimizes cold symptoms; shortens duration of illness; speeds wounds healing; promotes healthy gums; treats asthma; helps prevent cataracts; and protects against some forms of cancer and heart disease.

Vitamin D – aids in the body's absorption of calcium; promotes healthy bones; strengthens teeth; and may protect against some types of cancer.

Vitamin E – helps protect against heart disease, certain cancers, and various other chronic ailments; may delay or prevent cataracts; enhances the immune system; protects against secondhand smoke and other pollutants; aids in skin healing.

Vitamin K – reduces the risk of internal hemorrhaging; protects against bleeding problems after surgery; and helps build strong bones, and ward off or treat osteoporosis.

White willow bark (Salix alba) – relieves acute and chronic pains (back and neck pain), headaches, and muscle aches; reduces arthritis inflammation; and may lower fevers.

Wild yam – relieves menstrual cramps; may ease the pain of endometriosis; and reduces inflammation.

Zinc - fights cold, flu, other infections; treats a wide range of chronic ailments, from rheumatoid arthritis and underactive thyroid to fibromyalgia and osteoporosis; heals skin ailments and aids digestive complaints; may boost fertility, build healthy hair, and diminish ringing in ears.

Chapter 5. The benefits of essential oils

1. The secret formula for a happy and stress-free life

If most Aloepreneurs can enjoy a happy and stress-free life it is only because of the magic of essential oils. **Essential oils are highly concentrated liquids that are generally distilled from a variety of aromatic plants including the leaves, roots, grasses, stems, flowers, needles, twigs, fruit peels, and wood.** Essential oils are not the same as perfume or fragrance oils. Where essential oils are derived from the true plants, perfume oils are artificially created fragrances or contain artificial substances and do not offer the therapeutic benefits that essential oils offer.

Having essential oils in your home increased happiness, reduces depression and anxiety and actually can increase emotional contact with friends and family. Aromatherapists believe that essential oils can have a healing effect mentally, physically, and emotionally.

It's a well-known fact that flowers and plants have a positive impact on your mind and body and the same goes for their extracts. A separate study by Harvard University found the same results - increased compassion, feeling less negative, and more energy at work. In a trifecta of flower research, Texas A & M University found that flowers and plants in the workplace improve problem solving skills and increase creativity.

Essential oils have been used for therapeutic purposes for nearly 6,000 years. The ancient Chinese, Indians, Egyptians, Greeks, and Romans used them in cosmetics, perfumes, and drugs. Essential oils were also commonly used for spiritual, therapeutic, hygienic, and ritualistic purposes. More recently, **René-Maurice Gattefossé, a French chemist, discovered the healing properties of lavender oil when he applied it to a burn on his hand caused by an explosion in his laboratory.** He then started to analyze the chemical properties of essential oils and how they were used to treat burns, skin infections, gangrene, and wounds in soldiers during World War I. In 1928, Gattefossé founded the science of aromatherapy. By the 1950s massage therapists, beauticians, nurses, physiotherapists, doctors, and other health care providers began using **aromatherapy - the use of essential oils from plants for healing.**

These oils may be used in many different forms: they can be rubbed into the skin during therapeutic massage, added to a warm bath for relaxation and rejuvenation, or placed in an electronic glass or pottery diffuser or a clay candle to perfume the air and stimulate the senses. PubMed.org found that teens who received aromatherapy were significantly less stressed than those who received a placebo, indicating that it could be a very effective treatment for stress management.

Most popular essential oils

Again I am NOT a medical doctor or an aromatherapist. The information in this section should not be substituted for, or used to alter, medical therapy without your doctor's advice. For a specific health problem, consult your physician for guidance.

Roman chamomile (*Chamaemelum nobile*): antispasmodic, menstrual cramps, sedative, relieves anxiety/stress, insomnia, great for children (comforting, soothing), anti-inflammatory.

Clary sage (*Salvia sclarea*): antispasmodic, relieves menstrual cramps, aphrodisiac, relaxing, relieves anxiety/stress, labor pain management.

Eucalyptus globulus: expectorant, decongestant, beneficial for flu/cold season, clearing to the mind, energizing, bronchitis **(avoid with children under 2, use *Eucalyptus radiata* instead).**

Eucalyptus radiata: expectorant, this eucalyptus species is indicated for children with respiratory congestion, useful for colds and flu, antiviral.

Fennel (*Foeniculum vulgare var. dulce*): digestive, menstrual irregularities, antimicrobial.

Frankincense (*Boswellia frereana*): strengthens the immune system (CO_2 extract), soothes inflamed skin conditions, cell regenerative.

Geranium (*Pelargonium x asperum syn. graveolens*): PMS, indicated for hormonal imbalance, antimicrobial, nerve pain.

Ginger (*Zingiber officinale*): digestive, useful to eliminate gas, constipation, relieves nausea, warming emotionally and physically, anti-inflammatory, relieves pain, immune modulator.

Helichrysum (*Helichrysum italicum*): cell regenerative, wound healing, anti-inflammatory, indicated for bruises and swelling.

Lavender (*Lavandula angustifolia*): calming, reduces anxiety, wound healing, burns, cell regenerative, insect bites. reduces itchiness, general skin care, great for children, antispasmodic.

Lemon (*Citrus limon*): antiviral, great for cleaning home, cleansing to environments (room spray), uplifting, detoxing.

Lemongrass (*Cymbopogon citratus*): cleansing, antiviral, insect repellant, use for cleaning, antimicrobial.

Mandarin (*Citrus reticulata*): calming, great for children (can combine with lavender), slightly more warming citrus aroma.

Neroli (*Citrus aurantium var. amara*): relieves and reduces anxiety, antispasmodic, PMS, antidepressant, nourishing, postpartum depression, pregnancy/delivery.

Patchouli (*Pogostemom cablin*): antidepressant, anti-inflammatory, soothes the nervous system.

Peppermint (*Mentha x piperita*): relieves nausea, analgesic for muscular aches and pains, relieves/reduces migraines, energizing, antispasmodic, **do not use on children under 30 months of age.**

Rose (*Rosa damascena*): the queen of essential oils, cell regenerative, nourishing the emotions, aphrodisiac, relieves/reduces stress/anxiety, PMS.

Rosemary (*Rosmarinus officinalis*): indicated for respiratory congestion, bronchitis, colds/flu, expectorant, expands and deepens the breath, energizing, clears the mind, sinus congestion, circulatory stimulant.

Tea tree (*Melaleuca alternifolia*): antimicrobial, supports/enhances immune system, antibacterial, antifungal, antiviral.

Vetiver (*Vetiveria zizanioides*): cooling, grounding, astringent, useful for varicose veins, calming.

Ylang ylang (*Cananga odorata*): aphrodisiac, antispasmodic, antidepressant, nourishing.

2. <u>Methods of Application of essential oils</u>

1. Diffusion

Diffusing essential oils is one of the best ways to receive their therapeutic benefits. When we inhale essential oils, they go straight to our brain and are sent directly to other parts of the body to regulate and moderate. There are many essential oil diffusers on the market ranging in price and function. There are even USB diffuser you can attached it to your laptop or put it in your car. When you diffuse essential oils you can expect to experience the following benefits: mood or motivation enhancement, purify and improve air quality, increase alertness, boost the immune system, create a feeling of peace and wellbeing, reduce airborne pathogens, support relaxation, a great smelling home, insomnia or sleep disorders, stress or anxiety reduction, etc.

2. Massage or body oil –When using it with a carrier

A carrier is also known as base oil or vegetable oil, is used to dilute essential oils and absolutes before they are applied to the skin in massage and aromatherapy.

Recommended dilutions for massage oils:

- For infants and young children:

✓ 0.5-1% dilution = 3-6 drops of essential oil per ounce of carrier.

- For adults: 2.5% dilution = 15 drops of essential oils per ounce of carrier

    ✓ 3% dilution = 20 drops of essential oils per ounce of carrier

    ✓ 5% dilution = 30 drops of essential oils per ounce of carrier

    ✓ 10% dilution = 60 drops of essential oils per ounce of carrier

3. Baths

Add 2-12 drops depending on essential oil into a teaspoon of honey, whole milk, vegetable oil (carrier) or other dispersing agent then add to bath once you are in the bath. In general, aromatherapy full-body baths are useful to reduce stress/anxiety, alleviate muscular aches, pains, and tension and more. Check the properties of the essential oils you are using.

4. Steam inhalations

Place 3-7 drops of essential oil into boiling water, cover head with towel and breathe through the nose. Keep eyes closed. This is indicated for congestion in upper respiratory tract (cold or flu), sinus infection or sinusitis; enhancing respiratory function. A good example will be to use the lemon essential oil.

5. Aromatic spritzers

An aromatic spritzer is a combination of essential oils and water. Often a dispersant such as solubol is used to diffuse the essential oils within the water. Aromatic spritzers can be used as room fresheners, to cleanse the air, to uplift and energize, to scent space, or used during a massage or esthetic practice: e.g. sprayed on face cradles to keep respiratory passages clear. To make it, add 10-15 drops of essential oil (1-3 different essential oils) per ounce of water. Shake before using or add dispersing agent (e.g. solubol). This method is very good for room and air freshener, body sprays over which an aromatic blend will be applied, reducing undesirable odors in the air; enhancing breathing, and soothing a variety of emotional states.

6. Different types of inhalation

Direct inhalation refers to the technique of sniffing or inhaling an essential oil directly from a bottle, a handkerchief or a cotton-ball. Direct inhalations are most commonly employed for the relief of emotional distress and as supportive therapy for the relief of respiratory congestion or other respiratory ailments. Direct inhalations are also used for their effect on the nervous system. For instance when I have cold, I use a handkerchief or cotton-ball and I place 2 or 4 drops of peppermint oil on the handkerchief and inhale it two or three time before going to bed. I sleep well and wake up the following day with no cold. This method has always worked for me.

<u>17 ways to use essential oils at home</u>

1. **Refreshing kitchen surface cleaner**
   Add 2-5 drops Lemon directly to a damp sponge.
   Use it to wipe countertops and cutting boards to
   help combat bacteria and germs.

2. **Simple kitchen sink scrub**
   Combine 5 drops Bergamot, 5 drops Lime, 1/2 cup
   baking soda, 1/4 cup hydrogen peroxide in a small
   bowl and stir. Apply the mixture to the inside of the
   sink and scrub. Rinse with warm water.

3. **Laundry freshener**
   Add 5-10 drops Grapefruit, Lavender or Simply
   Citrus to a small, slightly damp washcloth; place it in
   the dryer while drying towels, sheets and clothes for
   a clean, fresh aroma.

4. **Trash can deodorizer**
   Add 1-3 drops Stress Relief or Sweet Ambiance onto
   a cotton ball and place it on the bottom of the trash
   can to help eliminate odors and germs.

5. **Toilet rolls**
   Place 3-6 drops Joy or Relaxation on the inside of
   the cardboard tube of a roll of toilet paper. The
   aroma will fragrance the bathroom with every turn.

6. **Grout scrub**
   Combine 10 drops each of Lemongrass, Pine, Tea
   Tree, 1 cup baking soda, 3 tbsp. liquid dish soap and
   1 tbsp. white vinegar. Mix well, then place a small
   handful of the scrub on an abrasive sponge and
   clean grout.

7. **Simple carpet deodorizer**

    Combine 12 drops of Lavender with 1 oz. baking soda. Mix well and sprinkle the mixture over carpets. Let sit for 15-20 minutes, then vacuum.

    Alternatively, try Cleaning, Spring Garden or Uplift.

8. **Cozy aromatic fireplace**

    Add 5 drops Pine, Frankincense or Sage to a medium-sized, dry log. Leave for at least 15 minutes and make sure the essential oil has soaked in before adding the log to a lit fire.

9. **Remove cigarette smell**

    Combine 4 drops Rosemary, 4 drops Tea Tree, 4 drops Eucalyptus and 8 drops Lemon with 1 oz. water in a spray bottle. Spray liberally around the affected area. Shake well before each use.

10. **Outdoor furniture scrub spray**

    Combine 20 drops each of Juniper Berry, Lemon, Pine and 2 tbsp. white vinegar in an 8 oz. spray bottle. Top off with water. Shake well and spray patio furniture liberally, clean and scrub with a heavy rag.

11. **Fridge refresher**

    Combine 5-10 drops Lime, Grapefruit, Bergamot or Lemongrass to a small bowl of water. Wipe down the fridge or freezer with the water.

12. **Ant & pest away**

    add 2-4 drops Peppermint on a cotton ball and place in locations where you have had problems with ants or mice. The strong aroma will disrupt scent trails and discourage them from coming back.

13. **Shoo fly don't bother me**

    Place 2 cups dried flowers or potpourri in a decorative bowl. Sprinkle 10-15 drops Citronella over the dried flowers. Place in an area where you want to ward off flying insects.

14. **Sponge refresher**

    Sprinkle a few drops Lemon, Lavender or Blood Orange on your sponge. Place in the top rack of your dishwasher to disinfect and leave a fresh aroma.

15. **General purpose & disinfecting cleaner**

    Add 20 drops each Eucalyptus, Lemon and Pine, along with 1 oz. white vinegar to a 2 oz. spray bottle. Fill to the shoulder of the bottle with water. Shake well before each use. Can be used on glass surfaces, windows, kitchen counters, bathroom surfaces and inside your refrigerator.

16. **Bathroom refresher**

    Add 1-5 drops Grapefruit, Lavender or Simply Citrus to a cotton ball and place behind toilet.

17. **Windex replacement**

    Combine 12 drops Cleaning blend, 1 oz. white vinegar and 1 oz. water in a spray bottle. Shake well to combine. Use to clean mirrors and windows.

SECTION TWO

IMPROVING YOUR WEALTH

Another important part of the Aloepreneur Lifestyle is to live a wealthy lifestyle. When we talk about wealth, most people think about money. We the Aloepreneurs define wealth not in term of money but in term of abundance. Being wealthy means having everything in abundance including money and time. Wealth means you keep generating more money whether you work or not, you don't worry anymore about how much things cost, whether you can afford it or not, and the word "expensive" doesn't exist in your vocabulary. Wealth also means having more time to do what you want to do, you wake up whenever you want and go to bed whenever you like. You have more options in your life, you don't report to anyone, you're free to do whatever you want and like, you have total control of your destiny. In short, you have freedom and abundance for the rest of your life without ever needing a job again. This section features the Aloepreneurs' wealthy lifestyle. You will learn more about the principles of wealth, the secret of wealthy people, and other useful tips to fully enjoy this new lifestyle.

Chapter 6. The secret of wealth

1. <u>Wealth is not an event but a process</u>

Wealth doesn't happen in a day but it takes a series of actions in order to get there. The principles are so simple to learn that anybody can use it. Building wealth is like raising a child and you must take care of your child until he or she reaches maturity. Raising a child involves so many things to do such as feeding, bathing, changing diapers especially when they are younger, educating and teaching until they reach the age of 18. The same applies for your wealth: but the only difference you don't have to wait longer because your wealth as an Aloepreneur can be built in less than 5 years. I will share with you some of the principles many wealthy people have used to become wealthy today. Those principles are not mine; and they have always existed. They can be summarized as follows:

Step 1: Believe in yourself and have a burning desire

You won't believe that the secret of wealth lies in YOU and you can achieve wealth whenever you see yourself ready for abundance. The very first step on your way to wealth and financial success starts with YOU; and only you can unlock the doors of your wealth because the key is already in your pocket. You need to believe in yourself and you need to have a burning desire to achieve financial freedom. With no desire it will be impossible for you to attain wealth.

I want you to ask yourself this question:

"Why do I want wealth?"

_____

_____

_____

_____

_____

Try to think about it, see what are your reasons or goals. Because with no valid reasons it will be difficult for you to find your way. It's like driving a car with no purpose, because you don't know where you are going.

When you know what you want, and you want it bad enough you can now start studying the principles of wealth.

I don't know about what you want in your life but as for me, my burning desire is to help people and make a difference in the world. I love to see people smiling and being happy; I want to build schools and hospitals to help the poor and needy people; I want to be able to afford anything I want without worrying about the price; I want my family to live comfortably; I want to help needy families across the globe; I want to play an important role in my community; I want to help people achieve wealth and health. Whatever your reasons, you need to make sure those goals or reasons are valid.

Step 2: Save 10 percent of whatever you earn

After finding your reasons, the next step is to save 10 percent of whatever you earn. It doesn't matter the way you acquire your income, make sure it is from a legal activity. If you can acquire it through your job, it's fine! You don't need to have a very good job to be wealthy, because as an Aloepreneur you know in your mind that your job cannot make you rich, you're just working temporarily to use your income to build your wealth. Therefore your job shouldn't be done on a permanent basis. If you live in the US you are even blessed and lucky because you can find any job starting with the federal minimum wage of $7.25 an hour and become wealthy. We are going to cover how to do that in the next chapters. In short, pay yourself first before paying any bills, it's very important to do that if you want to achieve wealth. And Uncle Sam has well understood this principle; when you buy anything it takes its share first via taxes. So do the same for any income you earn, take your part and use it to create wealth.

Step 3: Live below your means

Statistics show that half of Americans are spending more than they earn. If you want to be wealthy you need to get rid of your bad habits and start adopting new ones.

- earned $5,000 a month and spent $4000 = Good habits

- earned $5,000 a month and spent $6000 = Bad habits

Most people think acquiring more stuffs will make them rich. *We buy things we don't need with money we don't have to impress people we don't like.* If you earn $5000 a month and spend $6000 you are not living below your means. It's important to have control of your personal finance.

If you have credit cards or a loan create a repayment plan.

Another thing you can do to control your finance is to establish a budget. **A budget is a plan used to decide the amount of money that can be spent and how it will be spent.** Take a piece of paper or a notebook and right your sources of income (salary, wage, commissions, royalties, etc.) your expenses (fixed expenses: rent, mortgage, car loan, cellphone bill, etc.; and variables expenses: utility bills, groceries, gas, etc.). However, don't make any expense if it's not in your priority list.

Step 4: Seek advices from competent people

Knowledge makes you wealthy, not money or possession; so knowledge is power. You must increase your ability to learn and invest in yourself. It's important to seek advices from those who are competent to give it. If you have an eye condition don't seek advice from the optician but the ophthalmologist (Eye Doctor), because opticians don't test vision or write prescriptions for visual correction and are not permitted to diagnose or treat eye diseases. The same principle goes for your wealth.

If Paul shares a business opportunity with you and you have questions or concerns, please ask Paul for more information; don't ask your spouse or friend because they don't know anything about your opportunity and their opinions do not represent any expertise. Most people have missed lot of opportunities because of asking questions to the wrong people. If you want wealth you need to approach a wealthy person or study wealthy people.

Step 5: Learn to make money work for you

The secret to make money work for you is to build an asset. An asset is anything that makes you money and pays you over and over and over again. If it doesn't make you money it's not an asset but a liability (takes money out of your pocket). Wealthy people when they earn their income they invest in assets and spend what is left but poor people do the opposite – they spend what they have and invest what is left. A person with a wealthy mindset will build assets first with the income she earns and use the income from those assets to buy stuffs or luxury while a person with a poor mindset will use her income to buy stuffs or luxury. Do you see the difference?

Good examples of assets include stocks, real estates, royalties, etc. For example if you invest in real estates, you buy an apartment complex and you rent it out. You will make money for the rest of your life. Another example is when you write a book, you will receive royalties (money from the book sale) for the rest of your life. When the Aloepreneur build their assets, they do it by building a Network Marketing Business. In the next section, we will cover it in more details.

Step 6: Protect your wealth from loss

After working hard to create your wealth, you need to protect it. Most people acquire insurance to protect themselves from major financial loss. Insurance is simply a promise of reimbursement for a loss in return for a premium paid. When shopping for insurance products, you should match your needs with what the product offers and seek out the best deal. A solid credit history is also important because insurers use credit information to price some types of insurance policies. You can buy insurance to cover all kinds of risks, but basic needs can be met with property, health and life insurance.

WARNING!!!

Don't waste your wealth after acquiring it, reinvest wealth in creating more income-generating assets, and let your assets buy stuffs or luxuries.

Step 7: If you make a mistake, think about what went wrong and try it again.

On your journey to wealth, you will meet obstacles and you will often make mistakes. This is normal and it doesn't mean you are a loser but a student who is learning. There is no need to be discouraged. If something doesn't work you don't quit but keep trying until the process work. The same principles have worked for many people and will work for you too. Find the problem, fix it and move forward in the process.

What the wealthiest people all have in common?

When you take the current top five wealthiest people in the world, you can see that they are all **entrepreneurs** - Bill Gates (Microsoft), Carlos Slim (Telecom), Warren Buffett (Berkshire Hathaway), Amancio Ortega (Zara), and Larry Ellison (Oracle).

Going into business is a common path among the wealthy. While there are plenty of doctors, lawyers and corporate executives in the $5 million-plus group, those who go on to become business owners tend to build an even higher net worth. **Their net worth is directly related to the assets they own and not the salary they collect.**

Entrepreneurship is no doubt the best way to become wealthy in the 21st century. Inside the 2015 Forbes billionaires list (a total of 1,826 billionaires), **1,191 members of the list are self-made billionaires,** while just 230 inherited their wealth. So it's never late or early to start your own business. Colonel Saunders founded Kentucky Fried Chicken (KFC) at age 65 and became successful; and Evan Spiegel who is the cofounder of Snapchat is the current youngest billionaire with an estimated net worth of $1.5 billion. No excuses!

Why everyone needs to own a business?

Out of 100 people that started working at age 25, by age 65...1 percent are financially independent and wealthy, 4 percent have enough money to meet basic needs, 22 percent are still working and cannot afford to quit, 45 percent depend on family for survival, and 28 percent depend on state pensions, social security, friends or charity. Do you have a plan to achieve better health and financial freedom? Which group would you fall into at age 65? The 28 percent, 45 percent, 22 percent or the 4 percent? Higher? May be the 1 percent that are financially independent?

Today, you can't rely only on one source of income – *your paycheck.* You and I know when you receive this paycheck and pay your bills nothing is left to really enjoy life. I don't have to tell you that your job is not an asset, because you know you can't sell it on eBay or rent it out. Why spend decades, the best years of your life, working away to build something that is not an asset? Don't you want to spend quality time with your love ones? Or are you telling me that you love your job so much that you don't mind building your boss's asset and forget to build yours?

In the 90s you can't expect the Chicago Bulls to lose a game when you know Michael Jordan is playing, the same goes for our economy: Today, you can't expect to win the game unless you are an entrepreneur. The winners of the game are the entrepreneurs. You don't need to have a PhD in economics to understand that entrepreneurs gets the lion's share of the pie. For example, when you work hard for your organization and you make them earn good money, do they increase your salary or wage? Be honest with me and tell me how many times you had $10 added in your wage or salary in the past five years. I bet you receive an increase of less than $10 or none.

Statistics show productivity in the US grew 80.4 percent from 1973 to 2011, enough to generate large advances in living standards and wages if productivity gains were broadly shared. But workers, on average, have not seen their pay keep up with productivity. Where has all the money gone? Of course in the pocket of your employer. Today, you can fight for a raise but I don't think you will have it. You can either take it or leave it; and if you decide to quit, the very next day someone else is going to take your job or your employer can simply transfer your job in another country for cheaper labor or completely invest in new technology and get rid of you. This is the sad reality of the game!

If you want to win, you better learn the rules of the game and work for it to become a winner. **Most people lose the game on purpose and they voluntarily accepted to lose the game because of their fears, ignorance, lack of dream, lack of preparation, lack of self-discipline and lack of self-confidence.** They never wanted to win the game and they always wanted to play safe that's the reason they always lose. This game is meant for people who have a dream, people who want to improve their life as well as the lives of others, people who want to be somebody, people who want to make their family proud, and then people who want to leave a legacy.

The winners always win because they understand the rules of the game and they know what to do in order to win. What you have to understand winners don't work for paycheck (money) but money works for them. When you accept that paycheck you have officially accepted to lose the game. You have traded your time for money and therefore from 9:00 am to 5:00 pm you are not anymore in charge of your own destiny because you have sold your soul, mind, body, and emotion to that person.

You are working so hard to make that person very wealthy and voluntarily accepted to spend 40 years of your life in doing so because you are constantly told you can't find better than your current situation. The truth is that you can restore your freedom, make your dream come true and achieve financial freedom only if you are willing to learn the principles of the game and apply it.

Millions of Americans are now embracing entrepreneurship by running their own business. Most people would rather work for themselves than for a job, and a great percentage think about quitting their jobs constantly. Entrepreneurs are making our economy stronger and they will always win the game.

You need to shift position if you want to win - *you have to be in the game!* Spectators pay to watch while players get paid to play; you see the difference! In life as in sports, you either pay for what you do or you get paid for what you do. You either get in the game or you watch the game!

How much do you need to live a comfortable life?

To live a comfortable lifestyle you need to earn an average monthly income of $12,183. According to Kathleen Elkins, a money reporter for Business Insider, in order to live comfortably in 15 major US cities while saving money you need to earn between 122,448 and 169,944 a year. This represent an average monthly income of $12,183. The highest paying job in America paid around $20,000 a month. Let's look at the different ways to earn at least $20,000 a month (or $240,000 a year).

There are several ways to earn around $20,000 a month:

1. **Working as a doctors or surgeons** – If you are very smart and willing to use 11 years and plus of your life to study how to become a doctor or a surgeon you can earn an annual mean wage of $234,950. Of all the

medical professionals, anesthesiologists take home the most coin, with an annual mean wage of $246,320, surgeons ($240,440), obstetricians and gynecologists ($214,750), and family and general practitioners ($186,320) all make a very nice living.

Obstacles:

Student loan+ study for 11 years + be a smart student
→ When you choose this path, your income is limited. If you stop working you stop earning and you don't have control of your time. Their income is taxed at a higher rate than any other form of income.

2. **Savings** – Another way to earn is through savings. The current US personal saving rate is 5.60% and for you to earn $20,000 a month in interest you need to have at least $4,285,714.29 in your bank or savings account.
   Obstacles: it takes longer to save up to $4 million. Even if you are 25 years old earning an annual salary of $40,000 with an annual raise of say 3% will have earned an estimated $3 million if you retire by age 65. This is another 40 years of working and earning. At the end of the day you can't even reach $4 million and need at least 40 years of your life.
   → When you choose this path, it means you are already rich. Why sacrifice 40 years of your life to enjoy less than 14 years of wealth (since life expectancy in the US was 78.8 years in 2012)?

3. **Investing** – You can earn income investing in real estates, stocks, etc. Here you need to already be wealthy to expect earning more than $20000 a month from your

investment. Besides that, you need to have a good knowledge of the markets and good financial skills.

Obstacles: Must be financial smart + Already wealthy+ Need financial skills.

→ **When you choose this path, it means you are already rich. This path will be difficult for the average people to follow.**

4. **Become a celebrity** – If you have a talent you can be a professional sport athlete, an author, a singer, etc. In other word, you need to be gifted or have already acquired the skills.

Obstacles: Must be gifted + be lucky+ Need more skills.

→ **When you choose this path, it means you are already gifted or have already paid the price to acquire your skills. This path will also be difficult for the average people.**

5. **Inheriting a fortune** – If you have a rich family member or relative, this can be your way to make more than $20,000 a month.

Obstacles: you have to make sure you have your name on the will, and be willing to wait for the death of your relative before enjoying your fortune.

→ **When you choose this path, you are sure to have a rich relative and have your name on the will. This path is also difficult for the average people to follow.**

6. **Owning a small business** – Starting a business can be very challenging when you have to look for a business ideas, raise money, apply for business loan when you know you have bad credit, and take care of costs such as renting, hiring, and paying overheads. All these can be overwhelming and statistics show that 90% of businesses fail in the first 5 years. Few businesses can actually grow to a big business to hire at least 500 people. You need to have a good product or service and sell more to make more profit to expect earning around $20,000 a month. In addition, you will need more money if you want to purchase a franchise.

   Obstacles: You have to do everything by yourself when you start your business, and chances are you may not reach your $20,000 income in your very first year.

   → When you choose this path, your income is limited. If you stop working you stop earning and you don't have control of your time because the business owns you.

7. **Starting a Network Marketing Business** – You can start your Network Marketing Business and make as much as you want. You don't need to have a college degree, experiences, you can start your business for less than $150, no employees, no overhead, training provided, flexible schedule, you can manage business from home, no selling involved, etc. And this is the income Aloepreneurs decided to pursue in order to achieve financial freedom. You will learn more about this business in the next section.

SECTION THREE

NETWORK MARKETING BUSINESS

We are now at the most important section of the Aloepreneur Lifestyle. When the Aloepreneurs talk about improving their health and wealth, through a unique business model, they mean Network Marketing. Most people don't understand Network Marketing and think of it as a DOOR-TO-DOOR SALES or "PYRAMID SCHEME". This section will provide you with the basics you need to know about Network Marketing and you will understand why we think it's the best way to build assets regardless of your education, experience, gender, religion, ethnicity, political affiliation, age, or disability.

Chapter 7. Network Marketing 101

1. <u>What is Network Marketing?</u>

Network Marketing is an effective business model that uses personal recommendation to promote and retail a company's products or services.

Paul Zane Pilzer, the "wellness guru" defined it as Intellectual distribution, he said: "Intellectual Distribution is the process of educating customers about products and services, typically items that they either don't know exist or don't know are now affordable."

To illustrate the concept of Network Marketing, let me ask you a question:

Will you buy a product from a stranger or your best friend?

Assuming that the product has the same quality and cost. Of course you will buy it from your best friend. This method of distribution is called Network Marketing, Multi-level Marketing (MLM), direct selling or Team Marketing and is based on personal recommendation. A Family member or Friend will be more likely to buy a product or service when that product/service was recommended by someone they know and trust.

Many Companies now use this method to reach their customers. Because they think it's more cost effective! The World Leader of Aloe is a well-established, structured Network Marketing Company, designed to enable you to develop your own Aloe Business or independent business. Instead of spending millions of dollars in advertising, the company generously rewards you for sharing its products and business opportunity with others.

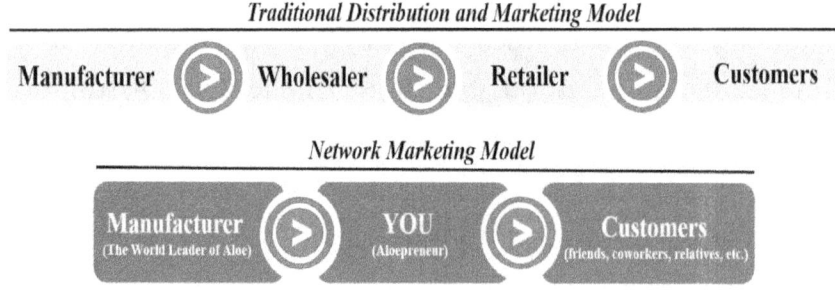

Traditional Distribution and Marketing Model

Manufacturer ▶ Wholesaler ▶ Retailer ▶ Customers

Network Marketing Model

Manufacturer ▶ YOU ▶ Customers
(The World Leader of Aloe) (Aloepreneur) (friends, coworkers, relatives, etc.)

Network Marketing is a simple and original approach without any intermediary such as exporter, wholesaler, and retailer.

As you can see in the figure above, you are the one between the Manufacturer (The World Leader of Aloe) and the Customers (your friends, coworkers, relatives, etc.). You won't find our Aloe products in traditional stores, like Walmart or Kmart because the Aloepreneurs sell their products directly to the consumers. Thus, it removes some intermediate costs and allows everyone to benefit from attractive prices.

And I personally think this activity shouldn't be called selling but sharing.

Selling is when you persuade, or influence someone to buy what you are selling and chances are the salesperson never use herself the product or service before selling it. Most of the time, the salesperson will proceed by pitching you about the products and try to convince you to buy. For example, I know a travel agent who never went to Paris but sells tickets to people who want to travel to Paris. He can tell you for instance: "this is the last ticket, if you don't buy it you won't travel!" (Using the Fear of loss approach to persuade you to buy.)

Contrary to selling, **sharing is when you're passionate about a product, service, or opportunity and you simply share your enthusiasm with others.** You are so excited to talk about your personal story and to share how the product has helped you and what you like about the product. You don't pressure or try to convince people to buy what you have, you only share your testimonial. If you remember we previously said that Aloepreneurs are individuals like you and I who use Aloe products every single day to improve their health and wealth.

2. <u>Advantages and disadvantages of Network Marketing</u>

<u>Advantages</u>

1. The Power of leverage

"I'd rather have 1 percent of the effort of 100 men than 100 percent of my own effort." J. Paul Getty. This quote describes the beauty of the power of leverage in Network Marketing.

Leverage means to gain an advantage through the use of a tool that gives you the power to earn more and more by working less and less.

A person can only work 24 hours a day but a team of 10 people can produce more than 24 hours a day (a maximum of 240 hours a day). For example, if you work alone and produce 10 hours a week and earn $2000, the day you get sick your income stops. But if you work with a team and you get sick you would still be earning money because your team got your back and gives you leverage.

In Network Marketing your earnings are based on your personal success, and your team's success. As you develop leadership skills, your compensation will reflect those skills. With Network Marketing, most of your income is made, without your presence or participation. Without leverage, you may work very hard, but your rewards are limited by the hours you put in. That's why employees or self-employed cannot afford to take long vacation or be absent from their work or business for a long period of time because they are income are limited and will stop immediately if they don't work.

2. Financial security (residual income and passive income)

Owning a Network Marketing Business offers you the possibility to enjoy both residual income and passive income. **Passive income is any money you make without doing any work.** Often times this money comes from investment of time, money or effort that you have already made. For example if you buy a rental house, you will receive passive income every single month. And the same applies for your Network Marketing Business, after building your organization or team you are guarantee passive income.

As for residual income, it means payments that you will receive after a sale. In general, these payments are agreed upon in advance and will continue long after the sale. A good example of this is royalties that someone gets for a book; he/she only writes the book once, but it can continue to be sold and resold again and again, which allows you to continue to make money from your work. And the same also applies for your Aloe business. Anytime someone buy a product on your online retail store, you get your share.

3. No college degree or experience required

You don't need a college degree or professional experience to own your own Network Marketing Business. You don't need to write a lengthy resume because it doesn't matter here. You must be at least 18 years old to start your own business. You WORK for YOURSELF but NOT by YOURSELF; your sponsor or upline will provide you with the training necessary to become successful in your business. You will learn almost everything on the spot and you will develop your experience along the way. No industry can provide you with a solid training in Personal Development except Network Marketing.

4. Being your own boss

Remember this is your life and nobody is going to make your dreams come true except you. If you want to make your dream comes true you have to take control of your life and not let anyone dictate you how to live your life. Jim Rohn says: *"if you don't design your own life plan, chances are you'll fall into someone else's plan. And guess what they have planned for you? Not much."*

Open your eyes and look around you, you may know a person who have worked for someone else in the past 40 years living now a miserable life or she is still working because she can't afford to retire. Why sacrifice 40 years of your life to enjoy only 40 percent of your paycheck? You can't even pay all your bills with your current paycheck, it's not 40 years later you will do so. It's time to prepare your transition to the Aloepreneur Lifestyle and become your own boss. Again, Jim Rohn says:" *let others lead small lives, but not you. Let others argue over small things, but not you. Let others cry over small hurts, but not you. Let others leave their future in someone else's hands, but not you.*" You deserve to live a quality lifestyle and you can do that with your Network Marketing Business.

5. Very low startup cost

In general, most people use their personal savings or borrow money with the bank to start a new business. Unfortunately, they end up losing their personal savings and become heavily indebted because the business is not successful. The marketplace is very competitive and you can't stand alone with those giant companies; they will squeeze you like an orange!

Statistics show that 50 percent of businesses fail in the first year and 98 percent fail within five years. There is no guarantee that your business will survive. That's the reason it would be smarter to partner with a successful multi-billion dollars company that has already paid the price for you by establishing themselves in the market. You build your company within a company.

Today you can start your Network Marketing Business with a minimum of $3.34 a day or $100 a month and we will show you how to do it in the next chapters. "*Network marketing is the big wave of the future. It's taking the place of franchising which now requires too much capital for the average person.*" says Jim Rohn. How many people can afford today the cost of a franchise (McDonald's or Subway)? Can you have at least $100,000 to start your Subway franchise? If yes, this business is not yours.

6. Stress-free business

Won't you be happy, if you work in a stress-free environment? **Owning your Network Marketing Business gives you so many benefits such as no inventory, no income ceiling, no employees, no commute, no website to design/ develop/ maintain and many more.**

When you start your business, you have your own online retail store which is already designed, developed and maintained for you. Your customers can go on your website (retail store) to purchase products. When they make a purchase, money is transferred on your debit card or deposited in your bank account. You can make more money as you want, you have control of your finances.

Just drive more people to your online store. You don't have to worry about inventory, when a customer buy a product, the product is directly delivered to their home in less than 3 days. Your business is portable, you can work from anywhere. If you like working at the beach or home is up to you! You just need a computer or smartphone with internet and you can see all your business activities through your devices (computer or smartphone).

7. Personal development training readily available

One of the greatest reasons to own your own Network Marketing Business is personal growth. You will learn more about yourself and others. You will develop new skills such as public speaking, mentoring, coaching, how to make friends, etc. You will learn how to believe in yourself, you will have access to a positive environment where people talk about success and improving their lives. You will become a better person, a confident person, a positive person, a happy person and you will learn more about how to improve your health and the quality of your life. *"If you become teachable and remain so, a network marketing career will make you money. More importantly it will mold your character."* Said Jay Vandenhoff.

8. Tax benefits

Another reason to consider owning a Network Marketing Business is the tax advantages available to business owners. If you take your Network Marketing Business seriously, you may qualify for some serious tax advantages that are available to business owners, and in particular, home-based business owners. You may want to check it with your CPA or tax advisors for more information, but below is an idea about some of the deductions you may qualify:

- Meal and entertainment costs
- Home office deductions
- Ordinary business expenses
- Travel expenses
- Business gifts
- Computer, automobiles, and capital assets
- And more

The most important aspect of claiming your expenses and deductions is keeping adequate records. The IRS will suggest that you keep a separate bank account, make a record of all business transactions, and retain all your records. There are many softwares that can help you keep your receipts safe and one of them is Taxbot (www.taxbot.com). It helps you track your mileage automatically using the GPS in your smartphone and digitally store your receipts.

9. Equal opportunity business opportunity

Network Marketing is an equal opportunity opportunity. There is no discrimination and the opportunity is opened to everyone regardless of your age, sex, nationality, religion, political affiliation, etc. Every individual has the same chance to move up in the marketing plan and achieve its dream. Only Network Marketing allows people who come from a humble background to live their dream. Everyone has the opportunity to make something of their lives. You can be the person of your dreams.

10. Build a legacy to your children

A legacy is a gift you leave behind without expecting anything in return. You can also pass your Network Marketing Business on your children. All the time and effort you put in the building of your Network Marketing Business is not free because it will benefit your future generation.

11. Flexibility of time

This is the most flexible business you may have because you only work whenever you want, you have control of your time. You may decide to work today or not and nobody will complain or tell you what to do. You are in charge of your life. You can decide to work one hour a day and spend the rest of your day with your children. This is the business for people who say **"I don't have time"** because this business will give you the control of your time.

12. Quickly profitable

This is the only business I know you can start today and before the end of the same year recoup all your investment and make a profit. At your very beginning your income may not reflect a big check in order for you to quit your job but you can make an extra income to help you cover some of your monthly expenses.

13. International possibilities

Your Network Marketing Business gives you the opportunity to do business globally. You may have customers in another corner of the globe or a business partner in France or Japan, anywhere in the world. With the advancement of new technologies it has never been easier to do business globally.

14. Travel the world and drive your dream car

Most Network Marketing companies offer incentives like international travels or driving your dream car. In our company you can travel the world twice a year and qualify for a car. How would you feel when you know the car you drive every day is already paid?

15. Business mentoring program available

You may have already heard, when you own your Network Marketing Business **you work for yourself but not by yourself**. Your sponsor (the person who introduced you to the opportunity) or your upline (your sponsor or the person above your sponsor) is responsible to coach you and help you in your business. It's like having all the experts or business advisors on your side to help you succeed in the building of your team.

<u>Disadvantages</u>

1. It's not a job or a get rich quick scheme

You don't start your Network Marketing Business today and expect to make more than your day job income the following month. You have to take your time to build your business first and let your effort and time pay you after. It's not every time you will make money, there will be month in which you won't make any sales. But it's normal and it is part of the entrepreneur lifestyle especially when you just started your business.

2. It's a "never quit" business

Owning a business is a lifetime proposition. It takes three to five years to build your business. You can't start your Network Marketing Business today and quit tomorrow. If you do so, you will lose your credibility with people you know and you won't make your dreams come true. It's like a mayor of a small city who promises to build a bridge for the city and at the middle of the work he decides to abandon the project. What would be the reactions of your own people? A time will certainly come where you will feel like quitting but don't. The only way you can ever FAIL in Network Marketing is by QUITTING.

3. People will say "no" (rejection)

People will say "no" to you and especially your friends but don't take it personally. The best way to fight rejection is to work on your skills and show them results. When someone tells you "no" it doesn't means "no" to you but to the opportunity; the person doesn't believe that the opportunity can change her life or it may not be the right time for that person to do the business. You can go back after 6 months to invite the person again. The good news is that the more "no" you get the closer you are to the "yes".

4. People will disappoint you (disappointment)

You will invite people to your opportunity and they will give you their words but they won't come. That's the reason when you invite 10 people expect at least 2 or 1 person to respond.

5. You can't be distracted

This is a business and it's important to manage your time accordingly. When it's time to play, play hard but when it's time to work, work hard too. You need to be very organized and protect yourself from distractions or anything that can slow you down in the exercise of your activities. You have to remain FOCUS and you have to read or listen more to positive ideas (books or audiobooks) every single day and keep away from negative people or the news.

6. You can't hate people

You're in a 'people' business, it's your responsibility to learn how to get along with people. That's the reason it's important to work on yourself every single day to become a better person. We are in the attraction business, you need to be attractive for people to follow you or need to care more about people before they care about you.

7. You can't be pessimistic

People with low self-esteem tend to be more pessimistic towards people and this will be difficult for such people to make big in our business. Nobody wants to be around people who are negative or spend their time complaining about other people. We are in the business to give hope and help people make their dream come true.

8. You must be coachable

You need to be coachable and follow the system established. You can't change the rules and you can't reinvent the wheel every day. Whatever successful people did to succeed you are going to do exactly the same in order to succeed. You have to put your ego aside and work as a team.

9. You can't sell a product you don't use yourself
Contrarily to the salesperson we use our own products every single month before selling to others. It's important to share your testimonials of the products to others for your business to grow. Don't expect to sell without using the products.

10. You will work as a teacher and not a salesperson
Your mission is to educate and inform people about your products and opportunity. You will have to face very bad students who know the industry as "pyramid scheme". You have to be compassionate toward them and explain what you have for them.

3. <u>People Who Have Endorsed Network Marketing</u>

- **Emanuel James "Jim" Rohn**
  (September 17, 1930 – December 5, 2009) was an American entrepreneur, author and motivational speaker. *"Network Marketing is really the greatest source of grass root capitalism, because it teaches people how to take a small bit of capital, that is our time, and build the American dream." Jim Rohn*

- **Tony Robbins** (born **Anthony J. Mahavoric**; February 29, 1960) is an American motivational speaker, personal finance instructor, and self-help author.
  "What's beautiful about network marketing is you get all the benefits of being a business owner, without all headaches, and without the same level of risk. And so I think network marketing is amazing." Tony Robbins

- **Robert Toru Kiyosaki** (born April 8, 1947) is an American businessman, investor, self-help author, motivational speaker, financial literacy activist, financial commentator, and radio personality. *"Network Marketing gives people the opportunity with very low financial commitment to build their own income-generating asset and acquire great wealth." Robert Kiyosaki*

- **William Jefferson Clinton** (born **William Jefferson Blythe III**; August 19, 1946), commonly known as **Bill Clinton**, is an American politician who served as the 42nd President of the United States from 1993 to 2001. *Bill Clinton speaks to Network marketers: "You strengthen our country and our economy not just by striving for your own success but by offering the opportunity to others." Bill Clinton*

- **Paul Zane Pilzer** (born January 17, 1954) is an economist, social entrepreneur, professor, public servant, and the New York Times bestselling author of 11 books and dozens of scholarly publications. *"In today's world, working for yourself is actually the safer route, and working for corporation has become the riskier proposition." Paul Zane Pilzer*

- **David L. Bach** (born November 19, 1966) is an American financial author, television personality, motivational speaker, entrepreneur and founder of FinishRich.com. Bach has helped millions of people around the world take action to live and finish rich. *"When I read Fortune Magazine that Warren Buffet, the billionaire investor, was investing in direct sales (Network Marketing) I decided I was missing something." David Bach*

- **Bob Proctor** (born July 5, 1934) is an American speaker and is widely considered one of the greatest speakers in the world on the topic of getting rich. *"What you sow you reap. It's the law of nature. Network Marketing is perfectly aligned with that. You truly get exactly what you are worth. No nepotism, no favoritism. That's rare today."* Bob Proctor

- **Leslie Calvin "Les" Brown** (born February 17, 1945) is an American motivational speaker, author, former television host, and former politician. *"Network Marketing has produced more millionaires than any other industry in the history of the world."* Les Brown

- Other famous people that give great credit to network marketing include: **Richard Branson** (an English businessman and investor, founder of Virgin Group); **Tony Blair** (a British Party politician, former Prime Minister of the UK from 1997 to 2007); and **Donald Trump** (an American business magnate, television personality).

4. <u>Misconceptions about Network Marketing</u>

#1 Network Marketing is a Pyramid Scheme

There is no debate about it, Network Marketing is **completely different** to pyramid scheme. According to the Federal Trade Commission (FTC), *"There are multi-level marketing plans (network marketing) - and then there are pyramid schemes. Before signing on the dotted line, study the company's track record, ask lots of questions, and seek out independent opinions about the business...Pyramid schemes are illegal, and the vast majority of participants lose money."* However, it is important to know that there are companies out there that are operating an illegal pyramid scheme disguised as a network marketing program. The same way some colleges deliver mock degree (Fake Bachelor or Master degree) to their students the same way the Network Marketing industry is affected by bad companies.

Before you join a network marketing company make sure you can check off all 10 attributes:

1. The company has at least a 5-year track record and is growing.
2. The company has sales of over 100 million during the first 5 years.
3. The startup costs is under $500.

4. No hotel presentation, no inventory to carry.
5. The product is marketable to the public and to the business owner.
6. Purchases are covered by money back guarantee and eligible for returns.
7. A consumable product that is easy and fun for people to market.
8. The product can be used by men, women, children and the elderly.
9. The product is better and less expensive than buying it anywhere else.
10. You can leave your business to whomever you choose on death.

#2 Only the guy at the top makes the money

This is most true in Corporate America where the CEO makes more than 300 times the average worker, but not necessarily in Network Marketing. You can start your Network Marketing Business today and make more money than your sponsor (the person who introduced you to Network Marketing) if you are willing to put more time and effort than him or her. It's like martial arts, you can start today with a white belt and work your way to the top and reach black belt based on your own effort and performance. Every individual has the same chance to reach the top if he or she is willing to pay the price. **It is important to know that in Network Marketing your income is related to your effort not your position.** If you work more (growing your organization or team) you earn more if you work less you earn less. Network Marketing is one of the fairest business opportunity out there.

#3 Network Marketing is all about recruiting the most number of people

If someone invite you to join an investment scheme and there is no product or service involved, this should automatically be a red flag. This is an illegal pyramid – *a fraudulent moneymaking scheme in which early participants are paid out of money received from later recruits, with the final recruits putting money in and getting nothing back. In short, it is a system based on profits from recruiting rather than retailing.* But if someone invite you to try a product and you like it because it makes you feel better and look better, there is no problem joining that person to market those products. I don't think you will have a problem sharing your experience with others because the product works on you. So you don't join Network Marketing with an idea to make a million dollars instead you join to help other people live a happy life by offering them an opportunity where they can improve their health and wealth. Remember the famous Zig Ziglar *"You will get all you want in life, if you help enough other people get what they want."* This is a people business where the interest of your customers come first before yours. You will become successful only if the members of your organizations are successful.

#4 Network Marketing is a get-rich quick scheme.

Even though it's possible to achieve a great result in Network Marketing in a short period of time, you still have to pay the price. I have personally seen people earning over $50,000 a month in Network Marketing and that in less than two years. With the advancement of new technology and the popularity of social media, almost everything is possible; it has never been easier than it is today to reach a great number of people and run your business over the internet. However, you still have to put effort and time in building your Network Marketing Business. To illustrate this, let's look at the construction of a bridge, it may take several years to complete the project and the progress may depend on the resources available. Could you believe that it took over 13 years to build the famous Brooklyn Bridge but since its opening till now, the bridge is still earning money (toll) from drivers using it. The same principle applies for Network Marketing; it may take you time to build your business and you may not get the big check immediately. Remember, Network Marketing is not like a job. You don't get paid an hour or monthly. You get paid after building a solid business. After establishing your solid business you can now expect the big check. But you have to put in the time to develop your network and build it into a successful organization before you'll start to see a consistent stream of income. While you build your organization you may still receive an extra money but not enough to make you quit your day job.

#5 Network Marketing is like selling

This is a very common misconception about Network Marketing, most people think that Network Marketers are Salespeople. There is a huge difference between Network Marketer and Salespeople. A Salesperson works full-time or part-time for a company, while a Network Marketer owns his own business and works whenever he or she likes. Salespeople talk to strangers to sell their products, while most Network Marketers share their experience of the products to people they know or people who share a common friends with them (referrals). A Salesperson don't need to use a product before selling it, while most Network Marketers use their own products before sharing with others. When Salespeople fail to meet sales quota, they can be fired; while Network Marketer don't have to meet any quota. Salespeople receive a salary cap; most sales jobs limit your pay range based on the market standard. While Network Marketer does not cap how much you can earn. The harder you work, the higher your financial rewards.

5. <u>Famous excuses about Network Marketing</u>

There are two things you can make in Network Marketing: either **money** or **excuse.** You can never make both.

The only thing poor people can afford is called "excuse" because it cost nothing. Famous excuses I hear every day when I share my business with people:

1. "I don't have the money."
2. "I don't have a college degree."
3. "I don't have any knowledge of a special area"
4. "I don't have any knowledge of business"
5. "I don't have any experience."
6. "I can't give up my secured income."
7. " I have 15 years invested in my current position"
8. "I am scared"
9. "I don't like sales"
10. "I can't talk to people" I am afraid to be rejected.

Benjamin Franklin said *"He that is good for making excuses is seldom good for anything else."* Please don't be that guy!

The ones who find happiness are the ones who don't make excuses. If it's broken they fix it... If it's wrong they make it right.

6. <u>Facts and figures about Network Marketing</u>

<u>Network Marketing in the United Sates</u> (2014)

- Over 18 million people (18.2) were involved in direct selling. Estimated retail sales reaching $34.5 billion.

- Americans Involved in Direct Selling: 79% non-Hispanic and 21% Hispanic; 79% White or Caucasian; 11% Black or African American; 5% Asian; 1% American Indian or Alaska Native; 1% Hawaiian or Pacific Islander; 5% other or non-identified.

- Sales Strategy used: 71.5 % Person-to-Person; 22.4% Party Plan; 6.1% Other. Representatives by gender: 74.4 % Female and 25.6% Male.

- Network Marketing Businesses selling Wellness products represented 30%, followed by services and other 22%; home and family care 18%; personal care 16%; clothing and accessories 8%; leisure and educational 2%.

- Sales by census region: 37.4% South; 24.3% West; 20.5% Midwest; 17.4% Northeast.

<u>Source</u>: Direct Selling in 2014: An Overview. Direct Selling Association (DSA). <u>www.dsa.org</u>

Network Marketing in the world (2014)

- Global Industry: $182.8 billion. [$182,823 (USD millions)] Over 99 million people (99,724,641) were involved in direct selling.

- Regional sales: 37% America; 17% Europe; Africa and Middle East 1%; Asia and Pacific 45%.

- Top 10 global market: 19% United States; 17% China; 9% Japan; 9% Korea; 7% Brazil; 5% Germany; 4% Mexico; 3% France; 3% Malaysia; 2% United Kingdom; 22% other.

- Global sales by product category: 34% Cosmetics and personal care; 29% Wellness; 13% Household goods and durable; 7% clothing and accessories; 3% books toys and stationery; 3% utilities, 3% financial services; 35 other; 2% home care; 2% home improvement; foodstuff and beverage.

Source: Global Direct Selling - 2014 Retail Sales. The World Federation of Direct Selling Associations (WFDSA). www.wfdsa.org

Network Marketing and other industries in 2014 (Global Revenue)

Industries (2014)	NFL	Music	Video game	Movie	Network Marketing
Global revenue (in Billion)	12	15	46.5	88.3	**182.8**

As it is shown on the table, Network Marketing is the best vehicle to achieve financial freedom regardless of your education, experience, gender, religion, ethnicity, political affiliation, age, or disability. **"Network marketing is an industry with a truly unique concept that allows every individual an equal opportunity for success." Robert Kiyosaki.**

7. <u>The Wellness industry and Network Marketing</u>

Wellness can be defined as the quality or state of being healthy in body and mind, especially as the result of deliberate effort. Wellness is also about making healthy lifestyle choices. According to Paul Zane Pilzer, an economist known as the "wellness guru", the next millionaires are the wellness entrepreneurs. And Pilzer even gives us a better description of wellness as "the greatest industry on earth" in his book, *the new wellness revolution: how to make a fortune in the next trillion dollar industry*: *"the opportunity to make an incredible fortune by doing incredible good in the greatest industry on earth-wellness."*

Aloepreneurs are also wellness entrepreneurs, and we can't be more than happy to be part of this new revolution because wellness is one of the world's largest and fastest-growing industries. We know and strongly believe that we can leave a great legacy to our children and make a difference in our community. It's no doubt, investing in the wellness industry can be the surest investment one can make. Not only to increase the quality of your life but to achieve financial freedom regardless of the nature of the economy - bad or good.

In 2013, the market size of the global wellness industry amounted to more than 3.4 trillion U.S. dollars. The beauty and anti-aging segment was by far the largest, constituting around a third. The various segments making up the wellness industry are diverse and include, among others, healthy eating and weight loss, fitness, alternative medicine and the spa industry.

You don't need to be rich or poor to understand how good it is to feel better physically and mentally. Even in financial and economic crisis, people may decide not to buy stuffs but will always have money for things that can bring them peace of mind.

More people around the world have begun to recognize the importance of wellness. In America, baby boomers (people born approximately between the years 1946 and 1964) represent an important segment of the economy (they hold almost 60% of all wealth) and they don't like what aging is doing to them and are willing to spend money to slow the aging process.

We the Aloepreneurs, are very proud to be under the umbrella of the World Leader of Aloe and respond to the needs of this immense market. We are confident that our business will grow since there are lot of customers willing to buy our excellent and natural products. No one can stay aside when it comes to feeling better and looking better. Here is an idea about the global marketplace in the various segments of the industry:

- *Global weight loss and obesity, $672 billion in 2015.*
- *Global skin care products, the market is expected to reach $102 billion by 2018.*
- *Global fitness industry, $75 billion in 2014.*
- *Global nutritional supplements, $3.3 billion in 2015.*
- *Global personal care products, the market is expected to reach $630 billion by 2017.*

- *Global essential oil products: the market is expected to reach $11.67 billion by 2022.*

As you can see, there has never been a better time in history to own your own Aloe Business. Owning an Aloe Business gives you a strong competitive advantages over the rest because no one can beat the quality of our products. Being vertically integrated enables total control over all stages of production – assuring our customers receive consistent premium products time after time.

8. How people earn income in Network Marketing

There are two ways to earn income in Network marketing:

- retailing
- recruiting

Retailing - occurs when you share your products with others. For example, the Aloe toothpaste we use is a fluoride free toothpaste. When you educate people about the danger of fluoride on children, they will buy your products because they want their family to be safe. Another product we also use is the hand sanitizer which has a pleasant smell. Anybody who tries it always want to keep it and there are several products we can share with others and when doing this activity we are retailing. **In our business you can earn between 35 percent and 48 percent profit on all retail sales.**

Recruiting – occurs when you share your business opportunity with others. Your goal is to help the new recruits become business owners or Aloepreneurs so that they can also retail the products to others and recruit people. This is the most lucrative part of a Network Marketing business because the recruiting activity is almost similar to opening a retail outlet in a traditional business. If you open a store in Florida and another in Virginia and three other stores in different states it's more profit for you. The same applies for recruiting.

You recruit people and teach them to do the same so that they are able to grow their own organization. You all work as a team or family where each of you is his or her own boss. You work for yourself but not by yourself. You can recruit locally as well as internationally. Our business is currently present in over 160 countries; this is a huge market for you to serve.

Every business owner or Aloepreneur is responsible to grow his own business locally as well as internationally by recruiting quality people who are willing to use the products and share with others. The greatest advantage of Network Marketing you don't only benefit from your own effort but the effort of your own team too. That's why you need to spend more time with your team and train them. People who spend more time on training and educating others will make more money than anyone.

For example if you use the product and recruit one person in your organization every single month and train every member of your team to do the same, you will have **248,832 people** in your organization by year five. What you did was simply recruiting one person a month or 12 people a year and teaching them to do the same. Below is how your organization will look like in 5 year:

You

(recruit one person a month in a year)

Year one: 12 people

(12 recruits x12)

Year two: 144 people

(144 recruits x12)

Year three: 1,728 people

(1728 recruits x12)

Year four: 20,736 people

(20736 recruits x12)

Year five: 248,832 people

With everyone doing a little bit, your organization was able to grow exponentially. If everyone in your organization consume or sell at least $100 a month of products, you will have a total sales of **$24,883,200 a month (248,832 x100)**. Our company reward business owner between **5 percent and 13 percent team leading bonus**. Assuming you earn 5 percent team leading bonus, you will earn **$1,244,160 a month (5% of $24,883,200)**.

N.B: This is for illustrative purpose only. Your income will be based on your own performance and the effort of every member of your organization.

9. <u>The Power of Compounding in Network Marketing</u>

Most people are driven by an appetite for instant gratification; they just want things now. Instant gratification is the desire to experience pleasure or fulfillment without delay or deferment. Basically, it's when you want it; and you want it now. This could explain the reason most people couldn't make it in Network Marketing. Whatever they do, they want to be paid or rewarded now; while it takes time to build great things and enjoy the benefits. When you start your Network Marketing Business, you may not see the results now but investing a great deal of time and effort in building your team or organization will definitely help you reach your goals.

A good example to illustrate that would be: a person who is given the choice to have a million dollars now or take a penny now and double the amount every day for the next 30 days.

$1 million now or a penny doubling for a month?

Would you rather have a million dollars now or take a penny now and double the amount every day for the next 31 days? I bet you will choose the million dollars now option as 90 percent of people will. I would have made this choice myself a few years ago. But this would have been the poorest choice, because you would have lost over $9 million at the end of the 31 day period. Don't believe me?

Look at the penny calendar below. The simple act of doubling your previous day's investment can rapidly reap huge rewards thanks to the powerful concept known as **compounding.** The principle of compounding holds true for even smaller returns (though it will take longer than a month to make your fortune). This is why compounding is a core aspect of good personal finance and the reason why the rich get richer.

After 31 days 1 penny becomes over 10 million dollar!

Sunday	Monday	Tuesday	Wednesday	Thursday	Friday	Saturday
1	2 $0.02	3 $0.04	4 $0.08	5 $0.16	6 $0.32	7 $0.64
8 $1.28	9 $2.56	10 $5.12	11 $10.24	12 $20.48	13 $40.96	14 $81.92
15 $163.84	16 $327.68	17 $655.36	18 $1,310.72	19 $2,621.44	20 $5,242.88	21 $10,485.76
22 $20,971.52	23 $41,943.04	24 $83,886.08	25 $167,772.16	26 $335,544.32	27 $671,088.64	28 $1,342,177.28
29 $2,684,354.56	30 $5,368,709.12	31 $10,737,418.24				

Penny Calendar: An illustration of the growth of your investment in Network marketing.

Expect people to laugh at you when you start your Network Marketing Business because the very first years your income may not reflect a big check but if you keep putting the time and effort in building your team or organization you will definitely reach your goals.

SECTION FOUR

THE ALOE BUSINESS SYSTEM

The purpose of this section is to explain how we can help you make your dream come true. You may now have a basic understanding of Network Marketing but may not know how to build a successful Network Marketing Business. The most important asset of your business is the members of your organization and for your organization to be successful you need to have a simple system that everyone can understand and copy. You cannot succeed in Network Marketing alone; you must work with people. It's very important to have the right kind of people doing the right kind of job in order to expand your organization locally and internationally. However, the Aloepreneur Business System believes that the more people you help achieve their dream, the more chances you have to achieve yours. If you follow the Aloepreneur System you will definitely achieve your dreams.

Chapter 8. Building your Network Marketing Business

1. The Aloe Business System in 3 simple steps

This is a very simple system for building an empire, an organization that expands worldwide.

IMPORTANT NOTE: We earn our income through the sale of products and are not paid to recruit.

- **A "Point" represents our internal currency**
- Every Aloe product is allocated a certain number of "Point"
- **Minimum Novus Customer Personal Consumption** (MNCPC≈ .570 points and cost $100)
- **Minimum Assistant Supervisor Personal Consumption** (MASPC≈ 1 point and cost $130-140$)

Step 1: Personal use (Novus Customer)
Aloepreneurs are good consumers of Aloe based products. You want to be healthier first before sharing the products with others. You're your **OWN BEST CUSTOMER**. At this level you're called NOVUS CUSTOMER: You

consume a minimum of **$100 worth of products** every single month. This is approximatively **0.570 points** of Personal Consumption.

Step 2: Becoming an Assistant Supervisor

You need to accumulate a total volume of **2 points within 2 consecutive months** in order to become Assistant Supervisor. When you become Assistant Supervisor you can now earn at least 35% retail profit and 20% profit on personal recruiting. **You're now in business for yourself but not by yourself! REMEMBER you don't have to do everything by yourself because your upline or sponsor will help you reach that level.**

The BEST WAY to reach Assistant Supervisor is to either RETAIL or RECRUIT. If you recruit you will need only **THREE people** who WANT to be Assistant Supervisor: They will consume a minimum of $100 worth of products a month and you will teach and help them to also retail or recruit THREE other people; so that they can also reach Assistant Supervisor Level. You (.570 points) and your THREE people (1.71 points = 3 x .570 points) now provide a total volume of **2.28 points** (0.570 +1.71) giving you the opportunity to become Assistant Supervisor and be your OWN BOSS.

Step 3: Building a 4-point business

When you reach the Assistant Supervisor Level, you want to build your business on strong foundations because you want a business that will grow and last forever. That's why you must adopt and promote good business habits within your organization. One of the most important habit you want to have is to produce a business that create 4-point every single month. A business that provides 4-point every single month gives you financial security (immediate retail profits) and it opens doors to many incentives such as qualifying for your dream car, the annual bonus income ($4000-$1million) and all-expenses paid trips abroad, with spending money included (twice a year). The best way to create a 4-Point business is either RETAILING or RECRUITING. As an Assistant Supervisor, you will now CONSUME 1-Point YOURSELF ($130-$140 worth of products) every single month and if you decide to recruit, you will need only **SIX PEOPLE** who WANT to be Assistant Supervisor: *They will consume a minimum of $100 worth of products a month and you will teach and help them to also retail or recruit three other people; so that they can also reach Assistant Supervisor Level.* When they reach that level you teach them how to build their business on solid foundations (Building a 4-Point business).

4-Point Business = 1-Point (Personal consumption) + 3-Point (Retailing/Recruiting)

Repeating this process over and over will guarantee you success in your Aloe Business, you will naturally and automatically advance in the different level or rank available in the marketing plan without sweating. Always remember your goal as an Aloepreneur is to help many people becoming Assistant Supervisor (owning their own business).

Summary of the Aloe Business System

- Phase one: Personal Consumption (PC): $100/month
- Phase two: Business Creation: PC + 3 Recruits (Future Assistant Supervisors)
- Phase three: Business Development: PC ($130-$140) + 6 Recruits (Future Assistant Supervisors)

N.B:

- Novus customer PC is $100 and needs 3 Recruits to become Assistant Supervisor.
- Assistant Supervisor PC is $130-$140 and needs 6 Recruits to achieve 4-Point Business.
- A recruit minimum PC is always $100.

2. <u>What is the main goal of the Aloepreneurs?</u>

The main goal of the Aloepreneurs is to help many people become Assistant Supervisor or owning their Aloe business.

We believe in Zig Ziglar who said: *"you can get all you want in life, if you help enough other people get what they want"*. There is no need to focus on being at the top if you are not ready to help other people be at the top. That's the reason we strongly believe that by helping more people achieve their dream we can also achieve ours.

When you become Assistant Supervisor you are your own boss and you're on the right track to achieve success. Your retail sales profit is 35 percent and you earn 20 percent on every person you recruit. In general, when you become an Assistant Supervisor, you are now eligible to buy products wholesale. Everything is being taken care for you, your commission payments, handling customer relations, shipping product to your retail and wholesale buyers, and much more.

What's next after Assistant Supervisor?

When you help many people reach the Assistant Supervisor level, you will naturally and automatically advance in the different level or rank in our marketing plan. Below are the different level of position in our Marketing Plan:

Level 1: **Novus Customer** (enjoy 15% discount on personal purchase)
Level 2: **Assistant Supervisor** (accumulate **2-Point** of products within 1 or 2 consecutive months, your 1-Point of Product cost around $130-$140.)
Level 3: **Supervisor** (accumulate **25-Point** of products within 1 or 2 consecutive months)

Level 4: **Assistant Manager** (accumulate **75-Point** of products within 1 or 2 consecutive months)

Level 5: **Manager** (accumulate **120-Point** of products within 1 or 2 consecutive months, annual income: $20,000 - $25,000)

Level 6: **Senior Manager** (2 Managers, $30,000 - $35,000)

Level 7: **Soaring Manager** (5 Managers, annual income: $45,000 - $104,000)

Level 8: **Sapphire Manager** (9 Managers, annual income: $75,000 – $168,000)

Level 9: **Diamond-Sapphire Manager** (17 Managers, annual income: $140,000 – $228,000)

Level 10: **Diamond Manager** (25 Managers, annual income: $350,000 and plus)

Level 11: **Double Diamond Manager** (50 Managers, $5,400,000 and plus)

Level 12: **Triple Diamond Manager** (75 Managers, annual income: $9,000,000 and plus)

Level 13: **Diamond Centurion Manager** (100 Managers, annual income: $25,000,000 and plus)

Most Aloepreneurs reach the level 5 or Manager Position within 5 or 6 month on average. Your sponsor should be able to provide you with more details about the Marketing Plan and company policy.

3. <u>Understanding the Business-Building Cycle</u>

When we have understood the Aloe Business System, the next step is to take action. This is the practical steps for building your organization, the "do it" section. Now let's look at the different steps in more details:

1. **Step 1: Making a list of people**
2. **Step 2: Inviting**
3. **Step 3: Presenting**
4. **Step 4: Following up**
5. **Step 5: Enrolling or Sponsoring**
6. **Step 6: Training**
7. **Step 7: Building team**

1. Step 1: Making a list of people

The most important asset of your organization is your people. Building the right team or organization provide you financial security and peace of mind because if you don't work one day you know that your team got your back or if something bad happens to you and you find yourself in the hospital you can still make money.

Making a list consist of identifying the right kind of people for your organization. We want to work with people who want to become somebody and are willing to pay the price to improve their health and wealth. We don't recruit people for the sake of recruiting; we recruit you because you deserve working with us.

We don't talk to strangers, we don't call strangers, and we don't do door-to-door sales. We don't put ads in the newspaper, we don't do hotel meeting, we don't distribute flyers, and we don't do anything salespeople do. Remember we don't pressure or beg people to work with us. You can't force a pig to sing or you can't force a fish to walk. **We only work with people we know, our friends, our colleagues, our neighbors, our relatives, our acquaintances, and people we share things in common.**

We are looking for people who want to make an extra income on part-time or want to own their own business. We DON'T talk to people who earn over $200,000 a year, we don't talk to smart people, we don't talk to C.E.O, we don't talk to negative people or pessimistic people and we don't talk to unemployed people. We always talk with friends and their best friends.

People who can work with us can be best described as follows:

- People who are married
- People who have a job (at least annual income $15,000 and plus)
- People who have kids
- People who are interested to improve their health
- People who own a home
- People aged between 25 and 85 years old.

- People of influence like teachers, housewives, pastors, etc.
- People who hate their boss, their job, and their financial situation
- People who want to make their dreams come true
- People who are positive or optimistic
- People who are dissatisfied
- People who are looking to make extra money on part-time.

When you make your list, work with honest and trustworthy people, people you can trust and people you feel good doing business with. ALWAYS RECRUIT PEOPLE WHO CAN DO THE BUSINESS ON PART-TIME.

You can start making your list from your cellphone's contacts or friends on your social media (Facebook, Twitter, LinkedIn, etc.)

2. Step 2: Inviting

When your list of people is completed, the next step is the invitation. When you invite you must be brief and you don't explain anything or don't talk about any business opportunity. When you are a new recruit, your main responsibility is to become a messenger and not the message; let this book do the talking for you or set up appointments and your sponsor or upline will help you sell the opportunity. Your invitation should be short and quick (maximum one minute).

Invitation using this book

"You know Paul, I've always admired and respected you for your business sense. Could you do me a favor?" (Wait for 'yes') "I'm currently running a great business on part-time and I am doing a market research on potential partners, would it be OK if you fill a survey for me? You can find the survey at the end of this book and I will give you a call by next week to take it back from you.

"Hey, you know Janet, I recently came across something that got me really excited and I immediately thought of you. I'd love to share this book with you and have you look at it and give me your opinion. There is also a survey at the end of the book, could you fill it for me?" I will give you a call by next week to take the survey back from you.

"Hey John, listen I recently came across something that got me really excited. I thought of you right away. I know you're going to want to take a look at this book. There is also a survey at the end of the book, could you fill it for me?" I will give you a call by next week to take the survey back from you.

Invitation using your sponsor or upline

"Hey, John! I've recently come across something exciting and I thought of you. Since I am new and just getting started, would it be ok if I introduce you to my business partner to share more with you? This way, you'll get all of your questions answered, and this will help me to learn more as well"

Set up the appointment for a three-way call or if your sponsor live in the same town with you go to your friend home with your sponsor or upline.

3. Step 3: Presenting

As a new recruit you will never talk about business opportunity to anyone unless you get proper training. If you cannot use this book, your sponsor or upline will be the one to help you present the opportunity to your friends or people you know. **Your main responsibility as a new recruit is to set-up appointment and your sponsor will sell the opportunity for you.** At this early stage you are learning the process and your sponsor will help you in the whole process. The purpose of the presentation is to educate and inform the prospects or your friends about the best part-time opportunity in the world. Our goal is to provide them information that could help them make an informed decision. You never close a sale on your first interview, you must follow the whole process and you never do the whole process alone. There will always be someone who has been trained with you.

4. Step 4: Following up

The gold mine is in the following up. This is where you will take back the survey and analyses it. You will have an idea about the feedback of your prospect or friend, whether he or she want to do the business. If your friend or prospect need more time, we set up another appointment to hear from him or her later. If your prospect say "yes", the next step will be to set up the date for his or her enrolment. If the prospect say "no" to the business opportunity, recommend the prospect to use the products or ask for referrals. You can call back the prospect six month later and repeat the process again and see if he or she can be interested about the opportunity. ALWAYS set up an appointment after a follow up.

5. Step 5: Enrolling or Sponsoring

Your sponsor or upline will help your friends or prospect enroll in the program. And you will also be present to learn how the enrolment is done. Your friend or prospect will purchase his or her $100 worth of products. Your upline will teach your friend how to use the back office and order products.

6. Step 6: Business Planning Meeting

After enrolling the new recruit, the next step is the business planning meeting. Your upline will help the new recruit to set up goals and learn about the Aloe Business System, the products, the company policy, the business cycle, the importance of doing 4-Point every single month, the main goal of an Aloepreneur (always helping other people become their own boss), and other important issues.

7. Step 7: Building the new recruit team

The same process will be repeated for the new recruit: making a list, inviting, presenting, following up, business planning meeting, and building a team. And then repeating the same process over and over. As a new recruit, you will learn more with your upline or sponsor by doing more of such activities. You need to pay attention to every step of the process because you will also train the new recruits of your own organization.

4. <u>The Aloepreneur responsibility</u>

- You are totally responsible of your team
- You will train every member of your team
- You will recruit for new recruits
- You will sell the opportunity to everyone
- You will run every meeting
- You will build relationship with everyone
- You must expect to win and expect your team to do so
- You must use the system
- You must lead by example

5. <u>Our Prospecting Tools</u>

The Aloepreneur Business System has always encouraged and will recommend the face-to-face prospecting method. We strongly believe it's an effective way to respond to the needs of our prospects and educate them about our opportunity. We can meet them in their homes or online or on the phone if they don't live around. We don't believe on hotel meeting or opportunity meeting to educate our prospects. We always use a simple system that anyone can use and copy. Remember if no one can duplicate what you do, your company will have difficulty growing. Some of the prospecting tools we use include:

Three-way call: you can use the free service of Freeconferencecall (www.freeconferencecall.com). This is a good prospecting tool when your prospect and sponsor live in a different state; and you guys can all three meet on a conference call and present the business opportunity.

The Aloepreneur account in the USA is:

- **Dial-in Number:**(712) 775-7031
- **Access Code:**406-166

Video conference: you can also use the free service of skype (www.skype.com) and you can download the application on your smartphone or computer. Another cool videoconferencing tool is Appear.in (www.appear.in) that provides video conversations with up to 8 people for free. No login required and no installs.

The Aloepreneur Lifestyle Book: This is our main prospecting book to educate our prospects about the opportunity we have; and it gives them the chances to learn more about what we do. You can purchase a copy of this on www.aloepreneur.com. We recommend you to buy at least 6 copies of the book: one copy for yourself and five copies you will lend to friends to educate them about the business opportunity. Remember the more people you educate and inform about your opportunity the more successful you will become.

6. <u>Advices for our new recruits</u>

1. **Believe in yourself, your products and your opportunity**: You are more than what people think about you. You have greatness within you and you deserve to live the life of your dreams. You must trust your products, use them every single day and be proud to share your testimonials with others. You must believe in this opportunity because we have the best part-time opportunity in the world.

2. **It takes time to build your business**: there is no shortcut in this business, if you follow the Aloepreneur Business System, you will definitely achieve your goals. Don't listen to anyone who propose you something new, easier or quick to achieve your goals. You must trust, believe and apply the different steps of our system.

3. **Attracting quality people in your business**: the only way to attract quality people in your business is to work on yourself. Become a quality person, work on improving yourself every single day: be positive, friendly, excited, believe in yourself and behave like a leader. Recruit lot of people to increase your chance of getting quality people. Quality people have entrepreneurial skills and are willing to pay the price to achieve their dreams.

4. **Don't listen to the news or negative people**: We are in the attraction business and we are dealing with people every single day. It is important to protect our thoughts from negativity. People always want to be around positive people.

5. **Be focus**: Don't be distracted! Spend your time educating more people about the opportunity and train your team to do so. Spend more time on income generating activities (retailing or recruiting). Dedicate at least an hour in your business every single day.

6. **Educate yourself:** Work on improving your skills every day. Become a better person every day. Keep yourself informed about our industry and activities. Read books every day or listen to audiobooks (you can listen on YouTube for free, look for people like Jim Rohn, Tony Robbins, Les Brown, Zig Ziglar, Napoleon Hill, James Allen, Eric Worre, Robert Kiyosaki, Rhonda Byrne, etc.)

7. **Always ask for help**: your upline or sponsor is there to help you succeed. If you have any concern feel free to ask for help.

8. **Never prospect alone**: Never talk to someone about your opportunity unless you receive a proper training. Always have your upline or sponsor when presenting the opportunity to others or always have someone to train with you when introducing the opportunity to

others, this is the best way for new recruits to learn when they see what you do.

9. **Take your business seriously**: Love what you do because you are your own boss. Be organized and planned your day ahead. You don't report to your upline or sponsor. We all work as a team and everyone is responsible of his or her own business. We are a family and work as a team within respect and cooperation. Always add new people in your list every single day. We don't make excuses, you will do it, do it and do it until you win.

10. **Always be honest:** Be yourself and never deceive people because you want to make money. Your customers or team members' needs always come first before yours. You will always be there for your people and you will always help them when they need you.

11. **Never lend money to people who cannot afford to do the business:** Never lend money to anyone. If the person cannot find the money to do the business, it means he or she doesn't want his or her dream to come true. Don't waste your money on such people.

12. **Rules about running your business while working full time**

Rule #1: Don't quit your day job. Unless you fulfill this:

1. Establish an emergency fund: You save 6 month to a year of income before going full time. So that you won't panic if you don't make any sales.
2. Have a team and a consistent income: at least $5000 a month.
3. Prove that you can do the business and make a good living for your family.

- **Rule # 2: Don't do it on company time or with company resources**
- **Rule #3: Keep performing well at your day job** even though you have a side business (Take extra training and volunteer for assignments)
- **Rule #4: Don't solicit your coworker or clients** (conflict of interest)
- **Rule#5: When you're at work, your focus must be 100 percent on your job.**
- **Rule#6: Don't tell your boss about your business** (What an employee does in the evenings and on weekends is not the boss's business)

13. **Make friends every day and help them become their own boss.** Be that person who bring hope or solutions to others. Help others achieve their dream. Be like a teacher and not like a salesperson. Don't put pressure on people, share your story and products testimonials to your friends.

Bonus (testimonials)

We designed this section only for you. We could have shared with you some great testimonials about people who are currently earning millions of dollars, driving their dream car, living in their dream home, travelling the world, enjoying quality time with their love ones but we decided not to talk about them. We are more concerned about helping you build your own testimonial than talking about other people success. How we can help you make your dream come true is our NUMBER ONE PRIORITY. We strongly believe in YOU and we are certain you can SUCCEED. We will teach you whatever it takes to become successful in this business and promise not to let you travel this journey alone. We want you to fill the blank and write your own success story. You must first believe PROSPERITY, ABUNDANCE, and SUCCESS before you ever see IT. If ordinary people were able to change their life, going from nobody to somebody, and achieve their dreams, you can also achieve yours. Write your story as if money wasn't a problem and time wasn't a problem, as if you possess all the success resources.

_____ **Full name** _____

> ## City, state or country
>
> ## A brief description about yourself
>
> ## *eg Soldier turned # 1 earner*

Here is a good format to help you create your success story:

1. Who are you? (Share your background, a little about you, what you do)

2. Why you were looking for opportunity?

3. How did you hear about the Aloepreneur lifestyle? Why did you join?

4. What results have you seen/ hope to see?

5. What has excited you the most?

_____

_____ , _____
_____

_____
_____
_____
_____
_____
_____
_____
_____
_____
_____
_____
_____
_____
_____
_____
_____
_____
_____
_____
_____
_____
_____
_____
_____

Bonus

Conclusion

We are now at the end of this book, and we hope you have learnt something new. If there is anything you don't understand in this book, please feel free to let me know. I will be more than happy to help you. Here is my personal information:

Sponsor information

Name: _____

Tel: _____

Website: _____

Sponsor ID: _____

REMEMBER You can make a great extra income doing a great service for people. People need to look better and feel better. This is the BEST part-time opportunity in the world and there's practically NO RISK and people are "double-dumb" not to give it a try!

There are no excuses. You CANNOT use TIME as an EXCUSE because this opportunity gives you control of your time; you work whenever you want. You CANNOT use MONEY as an EXCUSE because if you live in America and earn the federal minimum wage of $7.25 an hour, you can save $3.34 a day and afford $100 per month. You CANNOT use LACK OF EXPERIENCE or business knowledge as an EXCUSE because we are going to teach you what you need in order to succeed. You are in this business for yourself but not by yourself. Whatever your reasons, don't be like those who live the life of excuses.

Before we let you go, we want to share with you this quote from the famous Benjamin Franklin who said: **"When the well's dry, we know the worth of water."** The same goes for our health: when we get sick, we understand the importance of being healthy. Don't wait to get sick to understand how important it is to take care of yourself.

Even if you are not interested on the business opportunity, THINK ONE MORE TIME ABOUT YOUR HEALTH. Ask yourself these questions:

Am I proud of my diet? Are my eating habits perfect? Am I eating at least 5 servings of fruits and vegetables per day? Do I feel comfortable in my own skin? Do I work out or exercise at least 6 times per week? Can I afford health insurance? Do I have a plan to improve the quality of my life?

If you don't make a change, won't the next FIVE years be the same as the last FIVE years? **IS THAT WHAT YOU REALLY WANT?**

Life is all about choices. The choices you make today will determine your future.

Choose wisely...

READER SURVEY

Please use a pencil.

Date: _____ / _____ / _____

The purpose of this survey is to help us better serve you. And we promise to keep your information safe.

First name: _____

Last name: _____

Email: _____ @ _____

Tel: _____

INSTRUCTIONS:

Circle your response or fill the blank using a pencil.

The following questions is about your health and beauty lifestyle.

1. Do you have any health insurance? **Yes   No**

   If yes, how much do you pay a month?

   $_____

2. Have you used Aloe based products before? **Yes   No**

If yes, which one? _____

3. Do you smoke? **Yes   No**

   Do you drink alcohol? **Yes   No**

4. Do you take any medications? **Yes   No**

5. Do you take any dietary supplements? **Yes   No**

6. Do you exercise regularly? **Yes   No**

7. Do you often feel tired? **Yes   No**

8. Do you often feel depressed or stressed? **Yes   No**

9. Do you eat 5 fruits and vegetables every day?

   Yes   No

10. How much money can you spend a day to maintain a

    healthy lifestyle? (Eating healthy, going to the gym, etc.)

    $1 $4 $5 $10 $15

11. If you were to choose, which one would matter most to

    you? **A. feeling better   B. looking better   C.Both**

12. If we could show you an affordable way to feel better and look better would you be interested to learn more about? **Yes   No**

13. Have you been in Network Marketing before?

Yes   No

If so, which companies?

_____

14. Is it...**Unimportant   Important   Very Important** to provide a healthy lifestyle to your family?

The following questions is about your financial lifestyle.

1. Current career:

_____

2. Spouse career:

_____

3. What do you like best about your job/career?

_____

4. What do you dislike?

_____

5. Are you planning to retire with your current company?

 Yes No

6. What's most important in your life?

 Work   Spiritual Life   Family

7. What are your top two?

_____

8. Is it…**Unimportant Important Very Important** to provide financial security for your family?

9. If money weren't an issue, what would your life look like in these areas?

Home: _____

Cars: _____

Travel: _____

Education: _____

Charity: _____

Hobbies/Recreation: _____

10. Do you have any savings account? **Yes No**

If yes, how much do you save every month? _____

Interest earned: _____

11. Do you have any other types of investment?

None   Stocks   Mutual Funds   Bonds

Real Estate Other_____

12. Do you have an emergency fund? **Yes No**

13. Retirement: (Age on track for)

You: _____ Spouse: _____

14. Ideal Retirement Age? You: _____ Spouse: _____

15. If we put together a program that allows you to retire at your **Ideal Retirement Age** would you implement that program? **Yes No**

16. Approximately how much money would you need to earn annually to live your dream life?

$_____

17. When will your current career pay you that amount so you can live your dream life? _____years.

18. How does that make you feel?

_____.

19. If your career won't allow you to live your dream life, what's more important to you?

Staying in your current career - or –

Being able to live your dream life?

20. If we show you a legitimate and realistic way to earn your dream income through helping people in a meaningful way, would you do it? **Yes No**

MONTHLY $ COMMITMENT TO BUILD YOUR WEALTH AND IMPROVE YOUR HEALTH

Would that be ok, if you commit **$3.34** a day or **$100** a month to build your wealth and improve your health?

Yes No

WHO ARE YOUR TOP 3 PEOPLE?

Who are the top 3 people you know who are responsible, have families, and would like to improve their health and wealth?

- **Name:**_____
- **Occupation:**_____
- **Tel:**_____
- **Name:**_____
- **Occupation:**_____
- **Tel:**_____

- **Name:**_____

- **Occupation:**_____

- **Tel:**_____

TEXT MESSAGE INTRODUCTION

Please send the message below to your 3 top people so that

they can also be introduced to the Aloepreneur Lifestyle:

"Hey, _____! I've recently come across something exciting and I thought of you. Since I am new and just getting started, would it be ok if I introduce you to my business partner to share more with you? This way, you'll get all of your questions answered, and this will help me to learn more as well".